NEGOTIATION
TECHNIQUES

(That Really Work!)

STEPHAN SCHIFFMAN

AMERICA'S #1 CORPORATE SALES TRAINER

Avon, Massachusetts

To DMS and JRS

Published by
Adams Business, an imprint of Adams Media, a division of F+W Media, Inc.
57 Littlefield Street, Avon, MA 02322. U.S.A.
www.adamsmedia.com

ISBN 10: 1-59869-827-3
ISBN 13: 978-1-59869-827-5

Printed in the United States of America.

10 9 8 7 6 5 4 3 2 1

Library of Congress Cataloging-in-Publication Data
is available from the publisher.

This publication is designed to provide accurate and authoritative information
with regard to the subject matter covered. It is sold with the understanding that
the publisher is not engaged in rendering legal, accounting, or other professional advice. If legal advice or other expert assistance is required, the services of
a competent professional person should be sought.
　　　—From a *Declaration of Principles* jointly adopted by a Committee of the
American Bar Association and a Committee of Publishers and Associations

Many of the designations used by manufacturers and sellers to distinguish their
product are claimed as trademarks. Where those designations appear in this
book and Adams Media was aware of a trademark claim, the designations have
been printed with initial capital letters.

This book is available at quantity discounts for bulk purchases.
For information, please call 1-800-289-0963.

CONTENTS

Acknowledgments

I want to take this opportunity to thank the many people that have been involved in the writing of this book. Primarily, however, I wish to thank Peter Archer who took the concepts and turned them into a meaningful document that will be used by sales people. In addition, my appreciation goes to Karen Cooper, at Adams, for her belief in our product. It is interesting to think about how a book is developed and the use that it has.

This book is really about sales people, and their ability to keep going, no matter what. I, of course, want to thank Anne, Daniele, and Jennifer for all their support.

Introduction

Everything in life is a negotiation.

Take it from someone who's been around for a while. I've spent decades observing colleagues, friends, acquaintances, and family. I've taught hundreds of thousands of people how to sell, and I've written more than twenty books about how to sell. I've had a lot of time to reflect on what I do and what all salespeople do—the good, the bad, and the indifferent.

From all this I've come to understand that negotiation isn't just another add-on sales technique, something you learn along with how to close a deal or how to make effective cold calls. *Negotiation is at the very heart of sales because it's at the heart of everything.*

That's the most basic truth I can offer you in this book. Everything else flows from that understanding.

Of course, some negotiation is very public. Pick up the newspaper or scan an Internet news page and you'll see dozens of stories about negotiations, whether it's in the Middle East between the Israelis and the Palestinians or in Detroit between the auto industry (or what's left of it) and the unions. These talks are being conducted by professional negotiators—people who depend for a living on their ability to deliver a win for their side. Sadly, they're often not very good at it.

But unremarked by news sources, every day millions upon millions of negotiations go on. They're over everything from buying a used car to a family's decision about what to have for breakfast. These negotiations are woven into the fabric of our everyday life.

Look at it this way: We live in a society of millions of people—billions of people on a global scale. All of us spend our days interacting with one another face to face, over the phone, and by e-mail or snail mail. And all of us want different things. Some of them are big, some little, some overlapping, some completely opposed to one another. In fact, sometimes we don't even quite know what we want. But we can be sure it's different from what everyone else wants. That's what makes us individuals.

To live together in a reasonably harmonious way, we have to find common ground between those different wants and needs. That's what I mean when I say that everything in life is a negotiation.

The problem is that we're not born with a negotiation gene. And most of the time, it's not something we're taught. When you started kindergarten, the teacher didn't say, "All right, boys and girls. Make a big circle on the floor. Today we're going to learn about how to negotiate for what you want."

Because of that, most of us have picked up negotiating techniques on the fly. In that respect, salespeople aren't any different from anyone else. And sadly, as I've seen over and over again when I've talked to groups of them, salespeople aren't any better at negotiation than the rest of us.

That's why I've written this book. Because I believe that if salespeople are going to be successful, they have to be better at negotiation. And it isn't just something you can pick up. You have to learn it. You need to understand the philosophy behind successful negotiation, and you have to learn the techniques for it. Once you do that, you'll start to see changes in the size of your commission, the number of sales you close, the number of prospects you turn into clients. Trust me on this: The payoff for learning this stuff is potentially huge.

Having conducted a lot of seminars, talked to a lot of salespeople, and written a lot of books over the years, I've evolved a pretty consistent set of principles that underlie what I do. You'll find them running throughout this book.

- Believe in yourself and in what you're selling
- Listen to the client
- Gather information about the prospect
- Use your time wisely
- Be creative

These are the principles on which my tactics are founded. If you don't master the principles first, the tactics won't work for you. On the other hand, if you keep these basic points in mind, you'll discover that all the tactics flow naturally from them. Like most things in life, it makes a lot of sense if you put it all together rather than trying to use bits and pieces of it.

One of the common phrases used in negotiation books is "win-win." I've used this myself in some of my books, but the truth is I don't really like it very much. That's because it begs the question that's at the heart of good negotiations: *What are you winning?*

This has always seemed pretty basic to me. In fact, I've never understood why so many "professional" negotiators seem to ignore it. If you don't know what you want to win, how will you know if and when you've won it?

So here's my first big tip to you: Right at the outset of any negotiation, big or small, ask yourself what you want to win. Once you answer that question, you're on your way to being a world-class negotiator.

—Stephan Schiffman
New York City
June 2009

PART

1

Before You Sit Down at the Table

CHAPTER 1

Ask the Right Questions

Bob, a friend of mine who happened to be a sales manager, decided that he was finally ready to buy some new windows for his house, so he called up several local vendors, and each sent a salesperson to his house to make a presentation. The windows he liked best turned out to be the most expensive of the bunch, but he was okay with the price and he was ready to buy.

So he called up the vendor and said, "Come on over, I want to do business with you."

The salesperson who had made the presentation returned to his house, and before Bob could say *one word*, he said, "You want a discount don't you? Let me give you 10 percent off."

Bob had been ready to buy at the stated price, but now he started thinking that maybe he *did* want a discount, and that maybe 10 percent wasn't enough.

"I don't know," Bob said. "Is that the best you can do?"

Over the next twenty minutes, Bob said very little. When the salesperson offered him 15 percent, he just shook his head. When the rep upped the discount to 20 percent, Bob grunted. By the end of this "negotiation," the salesperson had given Bob 45 percent off the starting price!

Can you imagine the reaction of that salesperson's boss when he learned of the transaction? Can you imagine how the salesperson's strategy cut into his company's revenue?

Discount or Negotiate

I wish I could say that this sort of incident is atypical, but sadly, it isn't. For too many salespeople, *negotiate* comes down to *discount*. In the case of the salesperson in the example above, he was giving away the store before he even had to—offering a discount before Bob asked for one. But the truth is, he probably didn't have any other weapons in his arsenal.

SCHIFFMAN **SAYS . . .**

Going into a negotiation is like going into battle. Each side wants to win. Just as in a battle, don't show your strengths too early, and don't use up all your ammunition right away.

Use tactics like discounting carefully and selectively to respond to the needs and concerns of the customer.

I don't want to ignore discounting. It can be a very powerful weapon in locking in a sale, and I'll talk about it in a later chapter. The problem is that too many salespeople think it's the *only* weapon. Rather than thinking about all the elements of the sale, they focus on just one: price. That defeats them before they even start.

When putting a deal together, I usually find that price isn't the real issue that's blocking its successful completion.

There are many others. But salespeople too often act as if once they've addressed the issue of price, they're done. Rather than discounting, they'd be better off asking more questions to determine what the real issues are that are confronting the customer.

Let's look at the situation with Bob and his salesperson again. The sales rep came into the room with the assumption that the big issue for his client was price. He thought he'd get a jump on the sale from the very outset by knocking down the price with a discount. But the biggest mistake he made was the assumption itself.

What, in fact, did Bob want? He wanted new windows—the salesperson knew that. But what the rep didn't know is *what aspect* of those new windows was most important to Bob. How could he? He didn't ask Bob any questions.

This is the first and most basic lesson I have to teach you about negotiation: *Don't assume. Ask questions.*

What else could be important to Bob about the windows?

- **How strong are they?** Bob lives in an area with seasonal high winds that might put special strains on the windows. Frequent hailstorms might shatter the glass. So he's probably concerned with the product's durability.

- **How easy are they to replace?** Bob is getting on in years and doesn't want the hassle of hauling around heavy, awkward window frames. He wants something that will slide into place with a minimum of trouble.

- **How available are they?** Who wants to schlep all the way across town to cart back some replacement windows? And if the local supplier goes out of business, Bob wants to make sure he can still get the windows.

- **How soon can he get them?** Winter's coming on, the nights are getting colder, and Bob doesn't want to wait a month for the windows to be delivered. He wants them as soon as possible.
- **How safe are they?** Bob's grandchildren come to stay with him periodically. He doesn't want windows they might easily slam on their fingers or glass that could shatter and injure them.
- **How weatherproof are they?** The winters where Bob lives are severe, and he wants windows that will keep out the cold and reduce his heating bills.

The salesperson didn't ask about any of these things. As a result, he didn't know what was important to Bob.

Asking detailed questions would have told him that all the issues listed above were on Bob's mind, and the rep was going to have to address them in his negotiation. Questions would have told him something equally important: Not only were these issues important to Bob, but they were important in a particular order.

Asking about Bob's needs would have given the rep a hierarchy of issues from which to start negotiating. He would know which things he could push Bob on and where he might have to give a little. In fact, if he'd asked enough questions he would have found that price came pretty low in Bob's ranking of needs, so the discounting tactic wasn't going to be especially effective in closing the deal.

Go back to what I said in the Introduction: Everybody wants something, but everybody wants something different. *As a salesperson, your first job is to figure out what the client wants.*

Let me give you another example. It illustrates not only why it's important to ask questions, but also why it's essential to ask the right questions. This story is from the dog food industry. Now, I don't own a dog, and I don't buy dog food. But I understand the passionate nature of people who own dogs and are deeply attached to them. That's the key to making sales to them.

A couple of years ago, the dog food industry did a study of who was buying dog food in order to segment their customer base. It seemed pretty straightforward: There were old dogs and young dogs and big dogs and small dogs. Customers seemed neatly divided into those four groups, and the industry based its marketing and sales strategies on them.

That all seemed fine until some perceptive analyst pointed out that it wasn't the dogs who were buying the dog food.

The industry folks who had commissioned the study thought about this for a while. Then they redid the study. But this time they focused on the *attitudes of the customers toward their dogs.* Again, they divided customers into four categories:

1. **Dog as animal.** People who fall into this category think of their dog as an animal that lives in or outside the house. They give it food to keep it alive and healthy. But they don't have strong personal feelings about the dog. In some ways, it's like a tool (albeit one that barks), so price is an important consideration—more important than, say, the quality of the food.

2. **Dog as pet.** Those in this group consider the dog part of the family. They have an emotional bond with it that goes beyond its practical use. Quality of food is somewhat more important than the previous group, since they want the dog to be happy.

7

3. **Dog as child.** Just as you wouldn't want your little girl or little boy to eat substandard food, the people in this group want their dog to have good, nutritious dinners. Price is much less important now, compared to quality (for instance, the amount of necessary vitamins and so on).

4. **Dog as grandchild.** Nothing is too good for these pooches. Money is no object. For people in this group, the food is all about quality and making the dog happy. For the dog food industry, incidentally, this is the most lucrative segment of its customer base.

Isn't it clear that if you're going to make a successful dog food sale, you have to know which of these four groups your customer belongs to? And wouldn't the easiest way of finding out be to start asking questions?

SCHIFFMAN **SAYS** . . .

A negotiation is about winning. But at the start of it, both sides have to understand what they mean by the word "win." For salespeople, winning means getting the sale. But good salespeople figure out what the customer means by winning as well.

To negotiate successfully, start by asking what your customer wants. You can't win until you know the answer to that question.

This is what I mean when I tell salespeople that many times they can be their own worst enemies. They don't ask questions. And if you don't know what's most important to your customer, you can't negotiate effectively.

The Real Deal

1. Negotiation for salespeople shouldn't just be about discounting.
2. To be a successful negotiator, you have to use a variety of tactics and strategies.
3. Never make assumptions about what your customer wants.
4. Figure out what the other party wants. That's the key to any good deal.

CHAPTER 2

What Exactly *Is* a Negotiation?

Do a quick scan of the Internet and you'll find a ton of sites dealing with negotiation and negotiation skills. Many of them promote one or another set of techniques "guaranteed" to win.

Now, no set of guidelines can guarantee a win every time. Sales fall apart for all kinds of reasons, some of which have nothing to do with you, the salesperson. But it's true that you can do a lot to improve your chances of winning. And the first step in that direction is to understand just what's going on during a negotiation.

It Takes Two to Talk

At its heart, a negotiation takes place inside a *relationship*. Like a lot of relationships, this one can be good or bad, old or new, but it's always there, surrounding the negotiation. You want to maintain and improve that relationship. After all, your object isn't just to make a one-time sale. You want this to be an account that will last for a number of years. That means you have to know what the customer wants from the relationship and supply that.

To use an old expression, you have to concentrate on winning their hearts and minds.

This speaks to something that salespeople sometimes forget: You can't negotiate with yourself. Like any relationship, this is between two parties, and both of you have to participate in it.

SALES SCENARIO

Let me give you an example of what I mean:

A couple of years ago, a sales rep I know was involved in a negotiation. The meeting went well, and the rep proposed a price of $100,000 for the units.

The company executive looked at him, leaned back in his chair, and said, "Sharpen your pencil and come back with another number."

Now, at that point the rep could have gotten up, gone back to his office, and pulled out a lower number. Instead, he said, "You've got to help me. I can't negotiate with myself." The exec thought about that and then the two of them sat down and worked out a satisfactory price. The answer the sales rep gave gained a small, deserved fame in sales circles.

The more complex the sale, the more both sides need to work at it. Because you can't negotiate with yourself.

If the essence of negotiation is a relationship, the second part is figuring out what each of you needs. I can't tell you how many times I've watched sales fall apart or fall short of what they could be because the salesperson didn't think to ask the customer what he needed.

In the last chapter, I explained the importance of asking questions. This might seem a bit odd since to many people negotiation is about making statements like "I'll give you X if you'll give me Y." But I believe that questions get you to the heart of what's at stake in negotiation: *What do you want to win, and what does winning mean to you?*

Once you've figured that out, you have to *find the right product.* Moreover, you have to find what your product does that the competition's product doesn't.

I believe strongly that when we sell we're selling commodities. That is, we're selling products that other people in our field are selling. So the first thing to keep in mind is that your product or service has to deliver the same basic things as comparable products in the marketplace.

If you're selling software that cleans up computer hard drives and makes them run faster, it had better do that job at least as well as all the other cleaning software on the shelves. If you're selling cell phones that have a better service contract than anything the competition has on the market, you'd better make that clear in your pitch. Otherwise, there's no reason on earth why anyone should buy it.

Years ago, Jack Trout and Steve Rivkin wrote a very influential book about branding titled *Differentiate or Die.* Their lesson is still valid; your product has to be different from the competition. Moreover, it has to fulfill a need. The more intimately you know your product, the more you'll be able to pitch to the customer what it can do for him. And the more successful you'll be in negotiating a deal.

Price Isn't the Only Thing

For some people, product comparison is all about price. They're completely focused on explaining to the customer that their widget costs fifty cents less per unit than the widget manufactured by the competition.

Sometimes price is a good point of comparison. But it's certainly not the only one. There's also quality, delivery time, longevity, and a host of other things. So before you start negotiating about price, find out if that's the most important thing to your customer. Imagine a scenario like the following:

SALES SCENARIO

Salesperson: Mr. Jones, before we talk about my company's product line, let me ask you a couple of questions. If you could pick three things to improve about the way your widget works for you, what would they be?

Mr. Jones: Well, I'd like to see the widgets show up on my shelf a lot sooner. Right now, it takes ninety days from the time I place my order to when they get to my warehouse. Sometimes even longer, especially during rush seasons.

Salesperson: Okay. Interesting. What else?

Mr. Jones: I'd like the widgets to come in different sizes and colors. My customers are getting tired of widgets that only come in white and all look the same size. It reminds me of what Henry Ford said about the Model T: "You can have it in any color, as long as that color is black."

Salesperson: Great. Okay. And finally?

Mr. Jones: I'd like to see an escalating discount, particularly when it comes to orders of 50,000 units or more.

Notice that in this little scenario, Mr. Jones does pretty much all the talking. At this stage, your job is to shut up and listen. At most, you just need to interject a few words to show you're paying attention.

But in his answer, Mr. Jones has given the salesperson some very useful information. The most valuable is not only *what's* important to him, but *the order in which* it's important. Generally, when people talk they tend to put those things that are most important or essential up front. So here's where the salesperson can ask some questions to confirm that for Mr. Jones the key quality he's looking for in his widgets right now is an improvement in delivery time. Once that's confirmed, the salesperson has a powerful weapon in his negotiations arsenal.

SCHIFFMAN **SAYS . . .**

Negotiating is about winning. I can't stress that too much. But it's possible for both sides to win, if they can find points of common concern. And that means cooperation as well as competition.

If you're both trying to win, you both have to work together.

Never forget that the relationship you're establishing is not only one between two companies, but it's also one between people. It isn't that you and Mr. Jones have to become buddies and go out for a beer together. In truth, you don't even have to like each other. But you *do* have to find a point of commonality, a point where your goals can be aligned with each other. This is the real art of negotiation: seeing beyond the surface differences between the two sides to the underlying points where your interests are the same. Once you've found that place, you can use the negotiation to bring out those common interests and make them the foundation of the deal.

The Real Deal

1. Negotiation is a dialogue. You can't negotiate with yourself.
2. You need to figure out what winning the deal means to you.
3. Price isn't the only thing to negotiate about. There's also quality, delivery time, and functionality.
4. The more complicated the deal, the more closely you and your client have to work together to arrive at an agreement.

CHAPTER 3

Get a Winning Attitude

I've been selling and training salespeople for a lot of years. Basically, my philosophy of sales isn't that complicated. If you've read some of my other books—and if you haven't, you should—you probably know a lot of it already.

- Put the customer first
- Ask and listen, don't talk
- Never slam doors
- Be organized and be persistent

There are other parts to it as well, but these are some of the most important. And along with those things, I'd also say, "Have some attitude."

Some books about negotiation techniques treat the process as if it were entirely a psychological game. They seem to think it's sort of mental chess, and the most intimidating player will win. I don't go nearly that far. I believe that most sales negotiations really are about something specific. In fact, often the more specific you can make the negotiation, the better your chance of winning.

SALES SCENARIO

A certain sales rep of my acquaintance was having a terrible time during negotiations. The purchaser felt he'd been ripped off by the rep's company, and he was determined to put up every obstacle he could think of to winning the sale. When the rep said, "Black," he said, "White." When the rep offered a discount, he said it wasn't enough.

Finally, when they'd managed to slog through the discussion enough to come to some sort of minimal agreement, the purchaser looked at the rep and said, "I assume you're going to do this *pro bono.*"

You could have heard a pin drop for a minute, while the rep reined in his temper. Then he decided to show some attitude of his own. Calmly he said, "Well, my daughter's an attorney. I let her handle the *pro bono* work in the family, while I handle the work that's done for a fee." Then he smiled.

That was enough to break the ice. The purchaser chuckled at the comeback and lost some of *his* attitude. And the negotiation was able to proceed to a successful conclusion.

Sometimes a little humor is what's needed to improve everyone's attitude and get things back on track.

But at the same time, there's no question that a big part of any negotiation is attitude.

There are various ways of expressing this, and we'll talk about some of them in just a minute, but right from the start I want to stress this point: If you feel good about your product

or service, you'll be a much stronger negotiator than someone who doesn't. Confidence is key. And that's something
you can't fake.

SCHIFFMAN SAYS . . .

The more you believe in what you're selling, the better you'll
be at it. And the more strongly you believe in your negotiating
position, the better you'll be at winning.

*In negotiating, attitude is key to winning. If you don't
have the right attitude, you can't win.*

Attitude among salespeople is a funny thing. Some of
them—the best ones—have it. They get up every day with
enthusiasm for their product line. They spend hours with
their customers, figuring out how to meet their needs. They
project winning ten feet in every direction.

Others know that attitude is a key to success, but they
don't quite have it. They believe that attitude isn't so much
about what you feel inside as it is about what you say or what
gestures you use. So they talk loudly, they wave their hands
around a lot, but every person they meet looks at them and
says right away, "Fake!"

These are the people who give used car salespeople a bad
name.

When you have the right attitude, your voice, your gestures, your tone, all will reflect your enthusiasm. You can't
get the voice, gestures, and tone first and expect the enthusiasm and energy to come later. So the first thing you need to
do is sit down and have a talk with yourself.

Ask yourself, what am I doing for the customer? What problem does she or he have that I'm helping to solve? How am I making their lives a little better, a little easier? Remember that a negotiation with a customer is generally about pricing, quality, delivery, or functionality. How could you affect any of these things to make your product better for your customer.

Sometimes when you're doing this, you'll have a eureka moment, when it all falls into place and you can charge into negotiations with all your guns blazing. Other times it takes a bit longer, and the right attitude comes a bit at a time. But if you're honest with yourself, you'll get there.

Show Your 'Tude

As I said, with the right frame of mind, some things like voice and tone will come naturally. Other things, though, can reflect your new confidence and be valuable tools in a negotiation.

Start with your clothing. When you walk into a negotiation with a customer, who are you going to take more seriously: the businessperson who's well dressed and groomed, with clean hands, polished shoes, and nicely combed or brushed hair? Or someone who looks as if he's been sleeping on a park bench in a rainstorm? I'll take the first one every time.

You don't have to look as if you've just stepped out of the pages of *GQ* magazine, but before you go into a meeting in which you know you're going to be bargaining, take the time to check your wardrobe. This is no time for informality.

At the same time, you need to know the culture of the company you're dealing with. You don't want to clash with them. The rule of thumb I use is this: Try to dress a bit better than the person with whom you're going to be negotiating.

Not so much as to be overwhelming, but enough to demonstrate the importance you put on this negotiation.

SALES SCENARIO

A friend of mine told me he was once part of a team that was trying to arrange a substantial deal for his company, one that would mean, potentially, millions of dollars in revenue. The day of the negotiation, he and a male colleague arrived at the offices of the company with which they were negotiating. They were ushered into the office of one of the company's top executives, who happened to be female, and her second in command, who was male.

The exchange of greetings went well, and the two sides sat down at the table and began to talk. To my friend's horror, his partner throughout the meeting refused to make eye contact with the female executive. Even when he was responding to a question or statement from her, he looked at the man. As far as he was concerned, the woman—the person who had the power to make or break the deal—might not have been in the room.

Not surprisingly, by the end of the discussion the executive was openly showing her annoyance. And also not surprisingly, my friend's company didn't get the contract.

The lesson: Always keep eye contact with the person to whom you're speaking during a negotiation. That applies both when you first meet her or him and during the discussion itself.

When greeting the person who'll be sitting on the opposite side of the table from you during the negotiation, a firm handshake conveys confidence. Nothing signals weakness and lack of enthusiasm more than a "wet fish" handshake. Grip the other person's hand firmly, shake it once or twice, and then let go. Keep eye contact while you're shaking hands.

Get the Right Tone

What you say in a negotiation is essential to winning, and I'll talk about that in upcoming chapters. But here I want to stress that what's also important is *how* you say it.

During most of the negotiation, you're going to be sitting and talking. Don't slouch in your chair. Sit in a position that's relaxed and comfortable for you. You want to strike the right balance between sitting at rigid attention (which is going to make you seem inflexible) and lounging in your seat (which is going to make you too informal). Avoid hunching over, since that conveys a lack of confidence, and you're all about projecting confidence.

Crossing a leg over a knee tends to show stubbornness, although crossing your ankles is okay, if a bit informal. Avoid crossing your arms over your chest; that shows you as unmoving (though there may be times in the negotiation at which you want to appear that way).

If you have papers in front of you (and you almost certainly will), avoid needlessly fiddling with them. The same goes for objects such as pens, pencils, coffee cups, and paper clips. Make your movements purposeful and direct.

If you're negotiating at a restaurant or if there are coffee and donuts on the table in the conference room where you're meeting, keep your eating and drinking habits neat and unobtrusive. No one wants to talk to someone with a piece of spinach stuck in his teeth or coffee stains on his shirt.

A big part of negotiation is necessarily about conflict. After all, as I said earlier, you and the client want different things, and those things are probably incompatible, at least on some level. Negotiation is about trying to find points of compatibility between your different needs.

But just because you're in conflict with the person or people sitting across from you doesn't mean you have to get angry or abrasive. In fact, if you do chances are you've lost control of the negotiation and the sale isn't going to happen. So remember, you're here to get the sale and build a relationship with the customer. Everything else is secondary.

Find a volume level loud enough that no one can accuse you of mumbling or being unclear but not too loud. In conversation, volume usually equals aggression. In some negotiating situations, there's a place for a larger level of assertiveness, but it's not the way to start a discussion.

When the other person is talking, listen with your whole body, not just your ears. What I mean by that is, lean slightly forward and look directly at them. It's a good idea to make small sounds or say things that indicate you're listening attentively. You can also take notes to show you're paying attention. Nothing stops a negotiation faster than one of the parties getting the idea that the other is simply following a prewritten script.

Have a pad and pen, and take notes while the other person is talking. This will not only help you remember the content of the discussion, but it shows you're listening. Your notes can later serve as the beginning of the draft of the contract.

Negotiation is a dialogue. Remember, you can't negotiate with yourself. So you've got to show the other party you're listening, even if you don't agree with what they're saying.

Repeat back, in your own words, the other party's main point before replying to it.

Finally, watch the other person's body language as well as listening to his words. How he sits, stands, and his tone of voice will give you a lot of valuable clues about how to win the sale. Is his posture confident or nervous? Open or closed? Are there any topics he seems to be avoiding? Keep your ears and eyes open at all times for these signals.

The Real Deal

1. The foundation of a good attitude is confidence in your product or service.
2. Dress and act like you want the deal to go through.
3. During the discussion, listen, and show you're listening with your body language, comments, and note taking.
4. Be very aware of the body language and speech patterns of the other party. These will give you hints about how to conduct the negotiation.

CHAPTER 4

They Want to Win

At one point in my career, I was involved in a negotiation over salary—not mine but one of my employees. The discussion felt as if it was going around and around and not getting anywhere. I was impatient and irritated. Finally, I snapped, "Fine! You tell me what *you* want!" And I got up and walked out of the room.

That was a mistake. The employee did tell me what he wanted, and that's the number we wound up going with. It wasn't the worst mistake I've ever made, but I lost something I could have won. I let my emotions get the better of my head and paid the price for it.

What this story should teach you—apart from the fact that I'm not perfect—is that in a negotiation there's no room for leaving things on the table.

Negotiation is combat. And in combat, if you give your enemy an opening, he's foolish if he doesn't take advantage of it.

Twenty-five hundred years ago, a Chinese general named Sun Tzu wrote down the principles of successful warfare. *The Art of War* has been continuously studied since. At first it was known only in the East. But in the past several centuries,

Western military and political leaders, including figures like Napoleon and Douglas MacArthur, have also taken lessons from it.

Some of Sun Tzu's chapters include:

- Look for strategic turns
- Use information to focus resources
- Gain the mental advantage
- Fight only the battles you can win
- Consolidate your gains

Sounds a lot like a manual for negotiation as well as for combat, doesn't it? Since the 1980s, many businesspeople have discovered that Sun Tzu's text can be applied to business problems. Some Japanese companies have even made the book required reading for their executives. (For more Sun Tzu's application to business strategy, check out *Sun Tzu and the Art of War for Managers*, 2nd edition, by Gerald Michaelson and Steven Michaelson. Adams Media, 2010.)

One of Sun Tzu's most important lessons is that to be successful in battle you have to seize the initiative. He writes:

"Generally, he who occupies the field of battle first and awaits his enemy is at ease; he who arrives later and joins the battle in haste is weary. . . . If the enemy leaves a door open, you must rush in. Seize the place the enemy values without making an appointment for battle with him. Be flexible and decide your line of action according to the situation on the enemy side."

The point here is that this is just what I allowed to happen. I let my employee take control of the discussion and seize the initiative, substituting his own proposal about salary for what I wanted to pay. At that point in the discussion, he had more energy than I did, and as a result he won.

As a salesperson, you want to win. That means, as I've said, you need to win the sale. Your customer also wants to win, but her definition of winning is different from yours. She might want a better price, a faster delivery date, a better service contract. If she sees an opportunity to get any of those things from you, she's going to do it. At least, you have to assume she will.

SCHIFFMAN **SAYS . . .**

Some salespeople tend to assume their customers are stupid. I don't know why—maybe it's arrogance, or maybe it's ignorance. But in negotiations, it can be fatal.

Always assume your customer knows what she
or he wants out of the negotiation and is
going to try any means to get it.

This isn't necessarily because your customer is sneaky or underhanded. She's simply trying to get what she needs from the negotiation in the best way she can. The danger is not that she'll eventually wind up with what she wants; after all, you want her needs to be met as well as yours. The problem comes when she's able to meet her needs at the expense of yours. Then a potentially win-win scenario is turned into an I-win-and-you-lose situation.

Remember as well that even as you're doing research on your opponent in order to put yourself at an advantage in the discussion, he's doing the same thing. He's trying to find out what presses your buttons, what points he can bring up that you'll have a hard time answering. He's studying your past patterns of negotiating so he can find the weaknesses in your tactics and exploit them.

Sun Tzu recognized that in war the enemy is ruthless. In sales negotiation, you need to be the same.

Keep Control

The key to avoiding this kind of problem is to keep control of the negotiation. And Sun Tzu, in the passage I quoted above, tells you exactly how to do that: You've got to take the initiative.

SALES SCENARIO

Let's take a look at how this might work.

Salesperson: I see that last year you took delivery of 16,000 units of our product and sold through your inventory in nine months. Your average monthly sell-through was 1,800 units, so why don't we increase your order for this year to 21,600 units?

Customer: No, I don't want to do that. I've been seeing a trending down of sales in the past three months. Besides, I don't want the added warehousing costs that I'd have to bear with a bigger order.

Salesperson: I've been looking at the trending information as well. I notice that there was a dip in the summer months, but then you come back stronger in the months leading up to the holidays.

Customer: That's true, but I don't want all that product sitting in the warehouse for months in the summertime, costing me money.

Salesperson: Well, here's something to think about. How about if we break this down into two orders—one with enough stock to last through August and the other, a bit bigger, to take you through the holidays. You don't have to take delivery on the second order until September, so you're not paying the warehousing costs until the product's ready to move.

Customer: That might work. But would I get the same discount on both orders?

Salesperson: Well, since we're bearing the warehousing costs for the second order here, I'd want to see you take a substantially larger number of units for that to compensate. How about if we say that you take 10,000 units for the first order, through August, and 15,000 units through the holidays.

Customer: Say 13,000 units for the second order.

Salesperson: Let's split the difference and say 14,000 units for the second order.

Customer: Sounds good.

Notice in this example that you actually came out with a total unit order above the one you proposed to start with. Like all good negotiations, this was a dialogue. But also notice that you took all the initiative and made all the key suggestions that moved it forward. When the customer gave you an opening by talking about the issue of timing, you had the data at your fingertips and were able to step in and seize the position. When he proposed the same discount on both orders, you had a counter suggestion ready.

If you hadn't been able to do that, where would the discussion have gone? Probably in the direction of a smaller order or, possibly, a bigger discount. The other point this example illustrates is that a negotiation is a complicated piece of machinery with lots of moving parts. The one who wins is the one who can keep track of all the parts and get them to move in a well-oiled fashion.

The Real Deal

1. Negotiation is combat, and you have to treat it that way.
2. If you show weakness during a negotiation, the other party will take advantage of it.
3. Information is one of your key weapons during a negotiation. The more you know about your opponent, the better positioned you are to win the deal.

CHAPTER 5

Stop the Discounting Madness!

Some time ago, I was called in for a consult by a company in the Midwest. The funny thing is their sales numbers were high. They were getting plenty of sales, but they were consistently falling short on their revenue targets.

I talked to a number of their salespeople and quickly discovered that the sales staff routinely discounted between 10 and 20 percent. They didn't even try to make the sale before beginning the discounting gambit.

I called the company executives together and asked if they were aware of this. They were. Then I asked, "Why?" Why were they only going after 80 to 90 percent of their revenue goal, when they could be shooting for 100 percent.

There was an embarrassed silence. No one—*no one*—knew the answer.

As you can see from this story, discounting has become the default tactic of many salespeople when they open a negotiation. They act as if price is the only thing that's important to the customer. Having made that mistake, they compound it with another: They assume that the only leverage they have is whether to discount and by how much.

SCHIFFMAN **SAYS . . .**

When you discount as your first move in a negotiation you can never get the price back to its original level. Once a company asked me for a day's worth of training. After I got there, they asked if I'd be willing to put in another half day.

I agreed to throw in that half day for free. In their eyes, the price I charged for one day was now the price for one and a half days. And it remained at that price level for the rest of the time I dealt with them. I did them a favor, and it backfired.

Discounting as a favor during a negotiation is a bad idea.

As I hope you've realized by this point, this is a false premise. The fact of the matter is, as a salesperson you can negotiate over any one of a number of things:

- Quality
- Delivery
- Price
- Functionality

In the case of the company I described above, the salespeople had been trained by their bosses to concentrate on the issue of price. The curious thing was that everyone in the company was focused on the *number* of sales they were making instead of *how much revenue* they were realizing from those sales. It's a classic example of how concentrating solely on price as a point during a sales negotiation can lead you down the wrong path.

Discounting certainly has its place in negotiation, provided you don't make it the *only* tactic you use. By discounting the right way, you get a better quality of sale. That may sound a little ambiguous, but it's true.

Look at it this way: When you maintain the integrity of your price, you're telling the person on the other side of the table that yes, you think this is what your product or service is worth. The price reflects the value you put on that product or service, and you're prepared to defend it. If you discount right off the bat, you're making a statement that what you're selling isn't worth that much—at least not as much as is reflected in the price.

The fact of the matter is, *anybody can discount.* But not everybody can do it right.

Let's assume that you've asked your customer some smart questions to find out what she wants. Let's further assume that her most important need centers on price. This is where discounting is a helpful tactic. But here again, too many salespeople stumble over *how* to discount.

Your customer starts the negotiation with a number in mind—what she's willing to pay per unit. You also need to start with a number in mind. This is important for several reasons. First, it allows you to calculate beforehand just how big a discount you can give and still maintain the company's profit margins. There's nothing worse that tossing out a huge discount on a sale and finding out that your company can't support it.

Second, having a clear number in mind allows you to control the negotiation. It means you're not merely reacting to whatever numbers your customer throws out there. To properly develop the negotiation, you should have a series of numbers to present. You want a sort of stairway of positions, starting with the lowest and progressing to your highest point at which you can discount and still maintain the needed margins.

SCHIFFMAN **SAYS . . .**

It's Negotiation 101 that you should start with the lowest possible discount. But that's not always a great way to go. After all, if you start by discounting too low, your customer may assume you can't really do anything for her and walk away. Start too high, on the other hand, and you have nowhere to go.

Start somewhere toward the lower end of the scale but not at the absolute bottom.

Combine Discounts with Other Things

Once you realize that discounting is only one of several possible negotiations with the customer, you widen immensely the range of tactics you can use. Because now you can combine discounting with other points.

One thing to note here is that the concessions shouldn't all be on your side. You want the sale—as I said earlier, for you the definition of winning is getting the sale—but there's no reason why you have to give everything away. You can balance things.

Notice that in this case study, the salesperson is in control of the discussion. He's the one who's deciding how to move the negotiations forward; he's the one who's proposing multipart solutions to the problem. The customer is reacting to the salesperson's proposals. That's the dynamic you want to establish. Whoever can control the flow of the exchange has a big advantage in the negotiation.

SALES SCENARIO

Let's imagine the following scenario:

Salesperson: You said earlier that you'd like to see a 40 percent discount on each order of widgets over 10,000 units. Right?

Customer: Actually, I'd like to see that discount more like 50 percent.

Salesperson: Well, that might be possible. But only if you're willing to take delivery in six weeks instead of four.

Customer: Six weeks doesn't work for me. Is that the best you can do?

Salesperson: How about if we meet in the middle? We'll do a 45 percent discount on each order of widgets over 10,000 units, with delivery in five weeks.

Customer: Yeah, that'll work.

Also note that the salesperson does not give something for nothing. Remember the case of my friend Bob, whom I talked about in Chapter 1. The salesperson in that instance started giving away the store on price immediately. All Bob had to do was keep quiet and look discontented with the offers.

But in the example above, there's a real exchange. Each side gives up something, and each side gets something.

This leads to another point: You can't negotiate with yourself. It's a two-way street.

SCHIFFMAN **SAYS** . . .

A negotiation is a dialogue. And a dialogue, by definition, is between two people. The other side has to participate.

If, during a negotiation, you find you're the only one talking, something's wrong. Open up the discussion and get the other side talking.

A basic way to open a negotiation that's closed is to do what I tell you over and over to do: Ask questions. For example, in the case study above, if the customer stops talking, stops responding to your suggestions, ask him a question. Say, "Mr. Jones (or Ms. Jones), how important is delivery date to you? Is it more important that you get your widgets by June 19?" This sort of thing forces Mr. or Ms. Jones to start responding to you on some level. That's key, because what you're trying to do is get them to break away from the status quo. You want them to buy what you're offering. And you can't do that until you know what to offer.

Fight for What You're Invested In

I've always found it a bit odd that salespeople will fight so hard over issues of discounting and pricing. Because this is one area of the product where the salesperson probably has very minimal involvement. The question of how to price a product is decided by executives who are usually very far removed from the street. They're concerned with how to make budgets work, determining cost of goods, estimating return on investment, and so on. So they set a price that works for them and for their spreadsheets.

So why does the salesperson make it the main object of his negotiations?

Anyone conducting a negotiation is going to be more invested in fighting for something she or he has been involved in setting from the beginning. That means the organization should make an effort to involve the sales staff in *all* aspects of the product. Of course, there are limits to this; salespeople shouldn't step on R&D's toes or try to do the Marketing Department's job. But the more salespeople know about how and why the products' parameters have been established, the harder they'll fight for these things during negotiations. And the more they'll win.

The Real Deal

1. Discounting is a tactic, not a strategy.
2. Use discounting in combination with other tactics to gain concessions from the client.
3. Never give something for nothing. If you're going to discount, make sure you're getting something in return.
4. Don't discount as a favor during a negotiation. It'll come back to bite you.

CHAPTER 6

Never Be Lied To

Let me clue you in on a little secret: Everyone lies.

Yes, even you. I know you're sitting there right now, shaking your head, saying, "Boy, Schiffman's really gone over the top on this one." But believe me, I know what I'm talking about.

Everyone lies, and we do it all the time. Between the time you got up this morning and right now as you're reading this, you've told at least a couple of fibs.

The truth is, we're socially conditioned to lie. We're brought up to be polite to our elders, nice to our peers, and to be good, responsible citizens. Unfortunately, that tends to mean a lot of lying. Sometimes, it's almost a reflex action, one we're not aware of ("I'm sorry, officer, I didn't see that stop sign back there"). Sometimes, it's more thought out. As I'm writing this, the news is full of a politician who had an affair. He lied about it to the media, to his wife, and quite possibly threw in some lies to his mistress as well. You can't really classify that sort of lying as an unconscious reflex. He knew what he was doing.

Lying is also an inevitable part of negotiation, as it is of most business dealings. That's a sad truth, but truth nonetheless. I don't recommend that you lie during your negotiating discussions (for reasons I'll make clear in a minute). But it's essential that you be able to recognize when the other person is lying.

Why Do We Lie?

First, we need to understand why we don't tell the truth. There can be lots of reasons:

- **To be polite.** As I said, we're generally brought up to be courteous, so when Grandma asks you if you like her homemade cherry pie, you say, "Yes." Because it would hurt her feelings if you pointed out that she left out the shortening and a stick of butter, so the crust is tough as an old boot. We lie sometimes in order not to hurt the ones we love.
- **To make ourselves feel better.** You're chatting with an attractive member of the opposite sex at a party, and suddenly the subject of age comes up. Without even thinking, you shave off a couple of years from yourself. Or you promote yourself from salesperson to sales director. Or you casually let slip that you went to Harvard—even though your degree was really from a community business school. We like to feel good about ourselves, and sometimes we give ourselves a little extra help.
- **To cover our shame.** Every one of us does things we're ashamed of. And many times it's just easier and less emotionally wrenching to pretend we haven't done them.
- **To gain an advantage.** This comes up a lot in a negotiation. In order to get the upper hand, especially if we're feeling threatened or challenged, we lie.

As I hope I've made clear, telling yourself that you'll never lie under any circumstances is at best extremely difficult. I'm not going to advise you one way or the other about whether to tell Grandma the truth about her pie crust or to be completely honest with the next potential date you meet at a party. What I will argue is that you shouldn't lie during sales negotiations.

This view is one I've spent a lot of years developing, and it's backed up by my experience. It's not born of some abstract devotion to morality. I'm not trying to sound better than everyone or more honest. As with all my advice, there's a sound basis of practicality behind it.

As I've said before, when you're negotiating, you are strongest when you're the most confident. That confidence has to be real. You can't take a deep breath just before walking into a conference room and tell yourself, "Okay, now I'm going to start believing in my product and in my position." *You have to believe in yourself and in your product all the time.* If you don't, you'll never be a successful negotiator. It's that simple.

Don't Lie to Yourself

When a negotiator lies, the first person she lies to is herself. Take a look at the following scenario:

SALES SCENARIO

Customer: I need 150,000 units in Hong Kong in two months.
Salesperson: Sure. That'll be no problem. No problem at all.

> **Customer:** Are you sure? My experience has been that it takes at least three months, given all the paperwork.
> **Salesperson:** No, there won't be any problem. I'm sure. We can handle it. There won't be a problem.
> **Customer:** Well, if you're sure. Did you check on this, as I asked when I brought it up before?
> **Salesperson:** Uh, yeah. I checked. No problem. Like I, uh, said.
> **Customer:** Who'd you check with?
> **Salesperson:** The logistics coordinator. She said it was fine. But she's, ehm, on vacation now. Otherwise, I'd call her back and double-check. She said it was fine.

There are several things to note here. First, the salesperson is doing what we might call Grandma Lying: He's telling the customer what he thinks she wants to hear. He doesn't want to admit that his company probably can't make the deal happen.

Second, the salesperson is compounding the lie by saying that he's checked out the situation with someone from Logistics. His speech patterns and hesitations make clear that he probably hasn't.

Third, and perhaps most important, the salesperson is trying to convince *himself.* On some level, he probably has succeeded. He's thinking, "Sure, it'll be tight making that delivery date, but we can probably do it, and anyway, it'll be Logistics' problem once I finish this deal. So I won't have to worry about it any more."

How can we tell from this dialogue that the salesperson is probably lying? There are some pretty clear signs.

Anyone who's played poker is probably familiar with the concept of the tell. It's a small change in physical behavior that gives a clue to the player's opponent about the player's hand. Liars usually have a set of tells. Among them:

- Sweating or shaking hands
- Increase in nervous behavior (finger or foot tapping, moving objects, etc.)
- Repeating
- Stammering
- Lack of eye contact
- Louder voice and/or faster speech pattern

Of course, some of these may be normal behavior for the person you're negotiating with. It's also possible that your opponent may have a different or more subtle set of tells. But observe their behavior closely when you meet them and during the negotiation. If you suddenly start to notice any of these features in your opponent, pay attention. Chances are that they are getting twitchy with the truth.

Finally, why is it bad to lie during negotiations?

There are three reasons:

1. Lying makes you less confident in your belief in yourself and your product or service. And less confident means less effective.

2. Lies beget lies. Once you start, you tell more and more to cover up the one you started with. And sooner or later, the whole edifice comes crashing down. If you lie often enough, it can become a habit.

(For some politicians, it's practically a religion. Remember Nixon and Watergate?)

3. Lies don't stay hidden. Sooner or later, the rubber hits the road, and whatever you agreed to in the negotiation is going to have to stand on its own. In the scenario above, the units are going to have to show up in Hong Kong in two months. If they don't, the salesperson's lie will be exposed and his relationship with the customer will be destroyed.

Lying in business is a self-destructive activity. Save your fibs for the next time your spouse asks you, "Do you think this dress makes me look fat?" or "Will you enjoy going to the wrestling match with me?" Keep them out of negotiations. They'll just make your life harder.

The Real Deal

1. Everyone lies. But big lies have no place in good negotiations.
2. Look for signs that your opponent is lying.
3. Avoid telling the client what you think she wants to hear. It's much better to be honest and straightforward.

CHAPTER 7

Draw Up Your Battle Plan

I don't want to scare you, but the truth is that you can lose a negotiation before you even walk in the room.

Not because your opponent has already made up her or his mind; if that were true, the negotiation wouldn't even be happening. But because you've neglected to prepare yourself.

Think of negotiation as a battle. Both sides have guns. But if one side has forgotten to bring any ammunition, there's no question about who's going to be triumphant at the end of the day. In the next section, I'll talk about specific negotiation tactics. These are the weapons you bring to the table. But for them to work, you've got to have ammunition. And in this case, *the most important ammunition is information.*

Know Thy Opponent

When you sell, you're negotiating with your client in order to solve a problem. The client is trying to find a solution to her or his problem and wants to know how you can help. So the absolute first step in any successful negotiation is to determine what the other side wants.

43

Of course, you can and should ask a lot of questions. But you may not get the answers you want or need to be an effective negotiator. As I made clear in the previous chapter, there's a lot of dishonesty in business, some large and some small. You need more objective sources of information.

Here are some of the things you should check out in the weeks and days before starting a negotiation:

Annual reports. Companies issue these to their stockholders. Usually they contain a message from the company's chief officer, a summary of activities during the previous twelve months, as well as some numbers for revenue, sales units, mergers and acquisitions, and so forth. The chief limitation is that annual reports tend to be PR tools. Their object is to make the shareholders feel good about where the company's at and where it's going. Nonetheless, you can glean some useful information by carefully reading the report. Look at what it doesn't say as well as what it does. Is the company expanding or contracting? Is its leadership stable, or is there a new crop of executives who've just been installed? What are its hot properties? Is it emphasizing consolidation or is research and development given a prominent place in the report?

Stock price. Publications such as *Value Line* and *Barron's* can given you a summary of how the company's stock has performed during the past year, along with recommendations for buy or sell. From this, you can glean something of the financial health of the company.

News. For each organization with which you're negotiating, start a file. Keep clippings and notes, whether they're from *The Wall Street Journal* or the Internet. You want to track any significant news stories about the organization. Search for stories about both the company and about its officers. And be sure to separate fact from rumor; in these days of Internet-based communication, not all information is equal.

Websites. Check out the company's website. It will tell you a lot about how the company wants to present itself to the public. It will also contain important information about the company's products and services—their extent, projected release dates, significant features, and so on. As with annual reports, remember that the website is the public face of the company, so examine it with a critical eye.

Once you've made a thorough study of these and other sources of information, you need to take the next step and get yourself ready for negotiation. This is a matter of psychological preparation as much as anything else, so be sure to do it someplace where you feel comfortable and you're away from the day-to-day pressures of work and home.

Sit down and draw up your battle plan for the negotiation. Your plan should include several elements:

- Objectives
- Resources
- Walk-away point
- Alternative to a deal

SALES SCENARIO

Sometimes your opponent's objectives may not come out until you're involved in the actual negotiation. If that's the case, you have to be fast on your feet and adapt to his or her goals.

At one time, I was involved in a lengthy negotiation with a company in Miami for one of my training sessions. They told me what they wanted me to do, and I told them the cost. They asked for a day or so to think it over and then called me back.

When I walked into the room, the first thing the company exec said to me was, "The number you gave us is way too high. That's more than we want to spend for this project."

The negotiation might have ended right there, since I'd assumed that price was the most significant objective they had. However, I thought about it while I counted slowly to five. Then I said, "Look, I'm giving you a cultural change in this company that will have a longer-lasting impact than the money I'm asking you to spend on it."

The exec smiled and agreed to continue our talk. I was able to figure out that his main objective wasn't the price, it was what he was getting for it. And that saved the negotiation.

Take the time to consider each of these elements very carefully. Structure your plan as two parallel columns, one for you and one for your opponent. In each column, note down the objectives and resources you each have. Then, at the very bottom, write down your walk-away point.

SCHIFFMAN **SAYS** . . .

Negotiation isn't like being on the school debate team. You don't win for scoring points. You have to remember that your objective is to win, and winning for a salesperson means winning the sale.

At all times in the negotiation remember that your object is to win, not to score points.

1. **Objectives.** Here you'll have to think through not just what you want to get out of the negotiation, but also what your opponent wants. Consider carefully the degree to which your interests and those of the person you're negotiating with can be reconciled.

Separate objectives into principle and secondary ones. For example, your client may tell you he wants a decrease in the cost of the warranty you provide for the product. But his main concern may be a slowdown in foot traffic in his stores. From that point of view, since his main objective is to get more customers into his store, pricing may be his underlying main objective.

2. **Resources.** This is an extremely important consideration, since you need to know how much you can spend in terms of discounting, extra service, and so forth. You also need to know how much your opponent is willing to spend. In a word, you need to know which of you has deeper pockets.

Tangible items such as money aren't the only things to consider under resources. Also put down your experience and that of the person who'll be sitting on the other side of the table from you. How many deals have they negotiated? How long have they been with the company?

To that, add determination. How much does each of you want to achieve your objectives?

3. **Walk-Away Point**. This is something you *must* know beforehand. At what point are you willing to walk away from the table? As far as your opponent is concerned, you can make an intelligent guess, but for yourself, you have to know.

Sometimes (in fact, a lot of the time) this is determined by the numbers. If you can't do the deal and still make your mandated profit or commission, it's time to stand up, smile, and say, "Well, I'm sorry we couldn't come to an agreement about this."

Be sure to distinguish this from the *tactic* of standing up during negotiations and acting as if you're going to walk out. Your walk-away point isn't a tactic; it's the real moment when the deal under discussion becomes untenable.

4. **Alternative to a Deal**. I'll talk extensively about this in the next chapter, so we won't discuss it here except to say that it's an essential part of your battle plan.

Going into a negotiation with a battle plan is key to winning. Not just because you'll know more than the other person, though that's an important advantage, but because you've thought through where the discussion is likely to go.

Remember what I told you earlier: One of the keys to winning any negotiation is to keep control of it. It's easiest to do that when you have a first plan and stick to it.

The Real Deal

1. Never go into a negotiation without a thought-out plan of attack, including your objectives, resources, walk-away point, and alternative to a deal.
2. The more information you can accumulate from different sources about the party you're negotiating with, the better.
3. Use that information to try to determine their objectives, resources, walk-away point, and alternative to a deal.

CHAPTER 8

What's Your Alternative to a Deal?

There are a lot of books written about negotiation. I should know. I have a whole shelf of them. Business schools around the country teach courses in it, experts run seminars in it, and so on.

I'm not a big fan of all this. To me, a lot of negotiation is just common sense. As I hope you realize if you've read some of my other books, I believe the principles I've developed over the past couple of decades about how to be a great salesperson can be applied easily to negotiation.

One concept that a lot of people talk about is Best Alternative to a Negotiated Agreement or BATNA. This is a term invented by Roger Fisher and William Ury in their 1981 book *Getting to Yes: Negotiating Without Giving In.* Since then, it's become a tool widely used by professional negotiators. I have to confess that I hate the term. I'm going to discuss it here because it makes sense and it's one of the weapons you need in your arsenal before you walk into the conference room to start negotiating. But I'm going to simply refer to it as Alternative to a Deal, or, for short, Alternative.

In addition, I want to make one very important point about it before I start discussing it: Many negotiators seem to think that the Alternative to a Deal (or BATNA or what have you) is the *only* tool you need in a negotiation. As I hope to persuade you in this and other chapters, I believe it's just *one* of the tools that you should have. It's a very useful measure of what you need for a deal to succeed, and it can be a powerful reinforcement of your position. But it can't be your only weapon. If it is, you'll find yourself walking away from the negotiating table having given up a lot more than you wanted to.

How to Figure Out Your Alternative

The simplest way to look at your Alternative is this: What happens if the negotiation collapses?

For example, suppose you're negotiating a deal for the sale of 100,000 widgets. Your asking price is fifteen cents per widget for a total price of $15,000. To warehouse the widgets for the three months you estimate it will take to get another deal if this one doesn't go through will cost you $10,000. So in this scenario, your Alternative is $10,000. If your client were to offer you less than $10,000, it would be cheaper to keep the widgets in the warehouse for three months.

Now let's add some layers of complexity to this example. Suppose you're trying to sell the same widgets to Company A. You've opened the bargaining with an asking price of twenty-five cents for a total price of $25,000. While Company A is thinking over your offer, Company B approaches you with an offer of twenty-three cents per widget for a total price of $23,000. But—and this is a significant "but"—they'll take delivery a month before Company A, cutting your warehousing costs.

Assuming your warehousing costs for the widgets are $3,000 per month, the deal Company B is proposing is *actually* worth

$26,000 (the $23,000 price plus the savings of $3,000 in ware-housing). Now you can go back to Company A and tell them the price of the deal is 26 cents per widget. Your Alternative is $26,000 because if Company A doesn't make the deal, you can always go to Company B.

What I hope you recognized from this example is that as soon as you establish a strong Alternative, you're in a much more powerful position in the negotiation. You know what will happen if the deal collapses and you have to do something else.

It's a form of comparison shopping. When you buy a house or a car or a computer or anything else that costs a lot of money (some people do this when they buy anything, no matter how much it costs), you shop around first. You compare quality, price, anything else that's important to you. Then you can pick out the product that works best for you. If it's a product you want to haggle about, you find the best quality for the lowest price and ask the other stores to beat that price and that quality.

What about Intangibles?

Of course, in real life nothing is ever simple. When you're trying to establish your Alternative before a negotiation, sometimes it can come down to more than facts and figures.

Let's suppose you've got a deal ready to ink with Company X for 100,000 widgets at twenty-five cents per widget. Along comes a representative from Company Y and says they'd be happy to take those widgets off your hands for twenty-two cents per widget. And then, Company Z lets you know they'll purchase the widgets from you for twenty-four cents per widget. We'll also assume that all three companies will take delivery in the same time frame.

Normally, your Alternative would be twenty-five cents for each widget, and you'd start your negotiations with Company Y and Company Z with that in mind. But let's also suppose that Company Z is one that you've got a long-standing relationship with. You don't know the other companies nearly as well, but Company Z has been buying widgets from you for years. If this deal falls through for them, they make it clear they'll turn elsewhere for their widget supplier.

This alters things quite a bit. Now you have to figure into the Alternative an estimate of the value of your relationship with Company Z. You have to balance that against the value of establishing a relationship with Company X or Company Y.

Well, I said this wasn't simple.

Often an Alternative can't be determined by comparing a competing offer because there *is* no competing offer. In that case, you still have to think of the consequences of the deal under negotiation not going through. What happens if you don't get the sale? Or what happens if you do get the sale but there are other consequences?

Someone I know was once offered an opportunity to set up a training program for a major company. Accepting the offer would put him in a strong position, because the firm was a major player. He thought about it and finally turned it down. Why? Because if he'd accepted, he'd be out of business for two years. By the time he became available for other training work, his reputation would have vanished, and potential clients would have moved on to other consultants. He had to weigh that against the benefits of the contacts and prestige he'd reap from this new training position, but in the end, he decided it wasn't worth it.

SCHIFFMAN **SAYS . . .**

Your Alternative should be based as much as possible on the numbers you get from your research and what offers you have on the table from other competing clients. But don't leave out the intangible elements as well.

Spend the time to put a value on your relationship with your client. What will it cost you to lose that relationship if you walk away from the deal?

Before you sit down and start negotiating, *you need to know what will happen if you do get the sale and what will happen if you don't.* Play out the worst-case scenario in your mind and think about some possible solutions. If you don't get the sale, is there someone else you might make the sale to? Is there another way of making the revenue for your company? If you get the sale, what will be your obligations?

Think about your opponent's Alternative. What is she going to do if the sale doesn't go through? Does she have another supplier? What kind of price are they likely to give her? How important is it to her to preserve your professional relationship?

All this comes down to the following three steps you should take before starting a negotiation.

1. Sit down and think of all the possible alternatives to the deal not going through. As much as possible, put a specific monetary value on each of these alternatives.
2. Among those alternatives, find the best scenario.

3. Keep that alternative in mind as your fallback position in the negotiation. That's your Alternative.

What I've outlined here isn't a magic wand that will save you in all circumstances. But it's an important tool. If you keep it polished and oiled, it'll help you win more often than you lose when you negotiate.

The Real Deal

1. Your Alternative to a Deal is a calculation of what happens if the deal doesn't go through.
2. The Alternative includes not only the price you negotiate, but also other costs (warehousing, warranties, legal costs, etc.).
3. Your Alternative may also include intangibles such as the value of your relationship with the parties involved.
4. Besides establishing your own Alternative, prior to the opening of negotiations think about your opponent's Alternative as well.

CHAPTER 9

Preparing Yourself

Among my friends and business associates, I'm notorious for having a bad temper. And there are times when it really comes out.

A while back, I was sitting in a room, trying to work out a deal for some training. I'd been driving all morning; I'd had to get up very early to start, and my eyes were red and felt hot. My mouth was dry, as if I'd been chewing sand, and I had the beginnings of a severe headache.

On top of that, the guy I was talking to kept going around and around the same points. Just when I thought we'd wound up something, he'd reopen it. Finally, as I began to hope we were getting somewhere and I could go off to my hotel room and take a nap, he suddenly leaped back to the point we'd started with and said, "I think we'll have to reconsider this."

That did it. I got up and slammed my briefcase on the table. "You're wasting my time," I told him, "and I won't take that from anybody. Don't call me again until you're serious!" And I turned and walked out. My hands were shaking so badly I could hardly drive. I found myself pounding the steering wheel, shouting at him even as I was alone in my car. Other drivers who noticed my antics began switching lanes to get away from me. Fortunately, I made it to the hotel before having an accident.

I don't tell this story with any pride, any sense of "See how I don't take any crap from anybody." In truth, the story marks a weakness, one that someone who spends any large amount of time negotiating with me is going to be able to take advantage of. But I'm no different from anyone else. I don't think I'm any more emotionally volatile. There are just certain things that set me off—in this case, someone who has no respect for my time.

Remember on the television show *Star Trek*, how the writers made such a constant contrast between the emotional human Dr. McCoy and the cool, calm Mr. Spock? Spock was from the planet Vulcan, where the natives were taught from an early age to suppress all emotion and concentrate on logic. Whenever the starship *Enterprise* ran into some interplanetary crisis, McCoy would start raging and shouting while Spock patiently figured out a solution. Most of us (or at least most of the people I hung around with) identified with Mr. Spock. But when things start to go wrong, when tension ratchets up and a deal in which we've invested a lot of time and emotional energy starts to go south, we act more like Dr. McCoy.

What Ticks You Off

Over the years, I've worked hard to get my temper to the point where it's more or less permanently under control. But it hasn't gone away. It's still there beneath the surface. The difference is that now I have a much better idea of what triggers it. And that means I stand a good chance of making it work for me instead of allowing it to control my actions.

Anger can be a very powerful tool in negotiations. *But only when you control it.* If you get angry without meaning to, you can blow the most carefully set up deal and throw a lot of hard work and time out the window.

So before you walk into a negotiation, as part of your preparation you need to review what triggers your temper. Again, this is going to take some time sitting alone, thinking quietly, away from stress, phone calls, and so forth.

Think back to all the times over the past year or so when you've been really angry. Make a list of those situations. Now review each one and ask yourself, "When did I start to become angry? Was it something someone said? Something someone did? Was it the fact that the room I was in was too hot or too cold? What about noises? Music playing in the background?"

Don't underestimate the number of things that can trigger a strong emotional response in you. Here are some common triggers:

- Eye contact (or lack of contact)
- Certain words or phrases
- Certain gestures
- Colors
- Sound
- Temperature
- Smell

Sometimes a trigger is not a specific thing, but rather a situation. For example:

- You're offered a deal you regard as insulting
- Your honesty or intelligence is called into question

■ You feel like you're the butt of a joke
■ Your opinions are dismissed out of hand

Make your list as comprehensive as you can. Remember that there's nothing silly about these triggers. Often they have their roots in your childhood experiences. You probably don't remember their original cause, but you can, with a conscious effort, recognize the symptoms when they start.

SCHIFFMAN **SAYS** . . .

Even if you make a great effort to understand your triggers and to control your anger during a negotiation, sometimes it just gets away from you. Sometimes the other party does or says something that sets you off. This gives them the advantage, since now you're thinking with your emotions rather than your head.

If you find yourself getting angry during a negotiation, try doing something to break up the pattern. Get up from the table, suggest a short break, take a drink of water.

When you're done with your list, review it. If possible, come back to it several times over the course of a week. You're dealing with very deeply buried situations here, and it's quite possible that it'll take some time to identify all of them.

When you're confident you've listed all (or at least most) of your triggers, now's the time to try to minimize the effect that any of them will have on you. Some of them you can address pretty easily. If you know that when you sit in a hot room without any windows you become very irritable very quickly, try to arrange the negotiation discussions for a room that has a good air-conditioning system and a couple of big windows. If you're sensitive to noise, check the environment beforehand to make sure there's not a rock band practicing next door.

However, you won't be able to remove all the triggers, particularly the ones caused by words or phrases or situations.

For example, I hate the feeling of being forced into a corner. During a negotiation, if the other party tries more and more to limit my options, every fiber in me starts screaming out to resist. I get sullen. Then I get angry. And if things go too far, I get up and walk out. Afterwards, I sometimes regret it, but by then it's too late.

If you have triggers like that—and I'm sure you do, because everyone does—you can't change them. They're a part of who you are. But you can recognize them.

Let's look at how this might work.

Sales Scenario

Client: I don't like the discounting structure we've set up here. I can only agree to an arrangement that gives me a 55 percent discount on orders of 5,000 or more units.

You: That's out of our possible range, but I might be able to consider a 45 percent discount on 8,000 units if you agree to take an additional 5,000 in the next ordering cycle.

Client: No, that's completely unacceptable. I want at least a 55 percent discount. I know you can do it.

> **You:** I don't think we could—
> **Client:** This is the same arrangement I've had with other companies.
> **You:** We're not—
> **Client:** The only reason I agreed to talk to you is that you said you could do better. If you can't do any better than that, I don't know how you stay in business.
> **You:** Excuse me. I'd appreciate it if you didn't interrupt me or question my integrity. That makes me irritated, and we won't get anywhere if we don't listen to one another. Let's stop for a few minutes, get some fresh air, and come back. I'm sure we'll be able to hammer out a deal if we're both willing to think the best of one another.

In this example, the client has hit two of your triggers: interrupting and questioning your honesty. Because these are triggers, you're going to get angry. That's a given. But because you *know* these are triggers for you, you can recognize them and take steps to defuse the situation.

It's possible, of course, that the client knew these were triggers and was deliberately trying to make you mad. But if she was doing that, you've effectively removed that weapon from her arsenal. You've shown you know what gets you riled up and you're not going to let it stop the negotiation.

Now you've got your battle plan drawn up, you've identified your list of triggers and done what you can to minimize their impact on you. It's time to walk into the room.

The Real Deal

1. You can't stop yourself from getting angry. But by learning what makes you angry, you can control it.
2. Understand your triggers for various emotions.
3. When someone pushes one of your triggers and you feel your emotions getting out of control, find a way to temporarily halt the negotiations so you can go back in with a clear head.

PART

2

Sitting at the Table

CHAPTER 10

Making the First Moves

For more than half a millennium, people have been playing chess. Thousands of books have been written about it, millions of people have devoted themselves in large part to the game, and it's been the subject of movies, plays, and even a Broadway musical. That seems pretty amazing for something that involves thirty-two oddly shaped pieces sitting on a black-and-white checkered board.

But part of the reason for its popularity is that chess is combat in miniature. It's been called the purest form of conflict. All the two players have is their knowledge of strategy and tactics and their understanding of chess psychology.

I don't claim to be a great chess player by any means. Certainly, I'm not like those grandmasters you read about every now and then or even like some of the people who play every day in Washington Square in New York City, rain or shine. But I like chess because of the lessons it has for successful negotiation. After all, as I've said, negotiation is a kind of combat.

One basic rule of chess is that with very few exceptions (one, really), you have to make your first move with a pawn.

The first couple of moves players make with their pawns set the framework for the entire game. Matches have been won and lost in those few opening moves with what is commonly regarded as among the weakest pieces in the game.

Open with a Pawn

Why should this be the case? Shouldn't you start with your strongest piece and try to get it into the game early?

In fact, the strongest piece in chess is the queen. And experienced players will tell you that it's dangerous—sometimes fatal—to get the queen out onto the board too early in the game. Very often, players hold back until the middle game or even the end game to develop the queen, bringing it out when most of the other pieces have already advanced to strategic positions.

There are several reasons for this strategy:

- The earlier you bring out your queen, the sooner your opponent will attack her. It's best to bring her out when she's in the strongest position to fend off these attacks.

- Part of the queen's power is her range of movement. You can take best advantage of that when the board's been cleared of superficial pieces. Otherwise, the queen remains cramped and can't be used as she should be.

- The success of a chess player depends on her or his ability to use pieces in combination. You can't combine the queen, your strongest piece, with anything until other pieces have been developed.

■ The queen can be moved out in the middle game when the tone of the game has already been set. She can reinforce a strong attack and very often make it decisive. Or she can turn the tide of an onslaught by your opponent, pushing his pieces back onto his own side of the board.

So what's the lesson in all this for negotiators? It's very simple: *Open with your pawn rather than your queen.*

In other words, don't start the negotiation with your strongest weapon. Keep that in reserve until you need it and until you can combine it with other tactics.

Let's look at how this works in practice.

SALES SCENARIO

You: First of all, let's talk about some of the features you'd like to see on our product. You told me when we spoke on the phone that you didn't like the color of the product very much.

Customer: Yes. It clashes with the color scheme we've set up for our fall displays. I'd like to see something that works with that.

You: I see. What range of colors are we talking about?

Customer: Well, the main colors for the displays are orange, brown, and green.

You: What about red? Could red work with that?

Customer: Yes, I think so.

You: Well, we could change the colors for our units to red, but this would mean some changes at the supply end. You'd have to be willing to take a later delivery date.

> **Customer:** How late?
> **You:** We're looking at a minimum of three weeks.
> **Customer:** Okay. I can live with that if we can get the colors to work together.

In this dialogue, you can see the value of starting with a relatively unimportant issue such as the color of the units. By finding out that you and your customer can come to an agreement on this point, you start the negotiation out on the right note. And you're able, in the next step, to use this point to get a concession on the delivery time, a much more important issue as far as you're concerned. By opening with a pawn, you've been able, in chess terms, to win a piece.

The Value of Combinations

Amateur chess players think about their moves one piece at a time. More experienced players, though, recognize that pieces and pawns work best when they can attack or defend together. A pawn can be far more powerful in combination with a bishop, say, or even with other pawns than by itself.

In the same way, when you're negotiating, rather than putting issues on the table and letting them sit there by themselves, use them together. Concede on a small point in order to win a larger question. Make the fulfillment of one condition contingent upon meeting another.

For example:

SALES SCENARIO

Salesperson: Let's talk about warranty for a minute. Naturally, we can offer a warranty on these units, but that will have to figure into the unit price.

Customer: Well, how much would that increase my costs?

Salesperson: You said earlier that you were looking to keep the unit price under $1.50. We can keep it at $1.45 per unit with a two-year warranty.

Customer: I was hoping for three years.

Salesperson: That's tricky. It would only be possible if we go to a price of $1.65 per unit and a speeded-up delivery date. Could you handle that in tradeoff for a three-year warranty and take delivery in two weeks rather than three?

Customer: Yes, the warranty's important to us, so that would be possible.

The salesperson in this scenario has used three elements (warranty, price, delivery time) to get a significant concession from the customer (a fifteen-cents-per-unit price increase and better delivery time). If she had just negotiated on price without factoring in the other two elements, it's unlikely she could have pulled this off.

Remember: *Combinations are more powerful than single pieces.*

At Least Win Something

Another chess concept that applies in negotiation is related to what's called winning material. In chess, "material" refers to the opponent's pieces and pawns.

Obviously, as I said earlier, some pieces are more important than others are. A queen is a lot more important in chess than, say, a knight or a bishop.

Occasionally, you and your opponent will have an exchange in which you're unable to win a valuable piece, but you wind up with one or two less valuable pieces. Experienced chess players regard these kinds of exchanges as useful. While it's true that you always want to capture your challenger's most important pieces, sometimes in an exchange it's useful to win some material, *any* material from your opponent. The fewer pieces she has, as a rule, the less maneuverability she has, and the better your chances of winning the game.

Applying this to negotiating, what I can tell you is that in the long run I've always found it more profitable to get something out of negotiation than nothing. There've been many times in negotiations when I've been confronted by a situation where a deal was about to fall apart. In those situations, I've worked very hard to pull *something* out of the negotiation, even if it wasn't nearly as important as my original objective. My philosophy is that it's better to get something, rather than lose everything I've worked for.

Getting something out of a deal has several advantages:

- It establishes a relationship with the other side. Once you have that relationship, once you've established that you can successfully exchange interests with one another, you're able to go back in the future and possibly negotiate for something else more successfully.

- Something is better than nothing. From a purely practical standpoint, I'd rather win something from a negotiation and justify the time and effort I've put into it than to walk away and get nothing from it because I couldn't get the Big Objective.

A chess player with a long-term view of the game regards *every exchange* as important, not just those in which she wins the piece she wanted to win.

SCHIFFMAN **SAYS . . .**

The best tactics in any negotiation are used in combination with one another to mount an effective attack. In chess, if you send a Knight to attack your opponent by itself, chances are you'll lose it. But if you send it in combination with a Bishop or a Rook, it can be devastating to your opponent.

Review the elements of your battle plan and see how you can deploy them in combinations during the negotiation.

The Real Deal

1. Start negotiations with less important points, and win some early victories; keep your big issues in reserve.
2. Use issues in combination with one another. You're strongest as a negotiator when you can link different points and make them work together for you.
3. It's better to win something, even if it's not that important, than to win nothing.

CHAPTER 11

How to Structure Offers and Counteroffers

Seen in its most stripped-down form, a negotiation usually consists of a series of offers and counteroffers. You start by putting on the table a proposal that you believe will solve your client's problem—whatever that problem is. She responds with a counteroffer, you respond to that, and so on.

Sounds simple, right?

Unfortunately, some salespeople don't grasp that the essential part of a counteroffer is that it has to *respond* to the previous offer. Imagine the following dialogue:

SALES SCENARIO

Salesperson: We can provide you with fifty hours of training in our program, plus an extra ten hours of follow-up. The base cost is $250 per hour, and we charge $150 per hour for the follow-up sessions. So your total cost would be $14,000.

Client: That's higher than my budget can accommodate. I can only spend $10,000 on this project.

> **Salesperson:** Well, as I explained, our base rate is $250 an hour and $150 for follow-up, and we're talking about fifty hours of training.
> **Client:** I'm sorry. I don't see how we can possibly do this.

The salesperson didn't *listen* to the client. All he did in answer to the client's counteroffer was repeat his original offer. He didn't respond to the client's basic point, which was that she didn't have that much money to spend.

Even if you decide to hang tough on a point and not change the terms you're offering—and there are a lot of times when you'll need to do that—your response to the client needs to acknowledge what they've said. And you need to offer a solution. If it's not lowering your price, find something else. Maybe it's fewer hours of training. Maybe it's something extra you can throw in along with the training. In any case, you need to show you're working toward a solution. Otherwise, the negotiation runs into a brick wall.

Building a Negotiation Pyramid

Thinking back over all the negotiations I've been involved in, I've come to understand that the process of offer and counteroffer has a pyramid shape. This is illustrated in Figure 11.1

Your offer starts by proposing a solution to your client. The offer is as comprehensive as you can make it, given the scope of your negotiations.

Their counteroffer will be equally broad and will reflect what's important to them. They may not respond to every point in your offer, but don't assume that what they haven't

Agreement

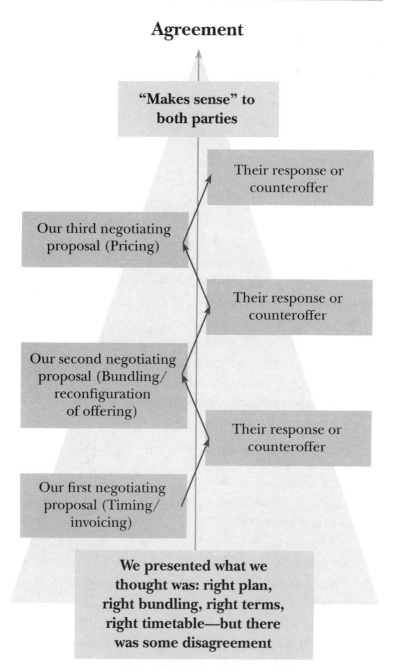

"Makes sense" to both parties

Their response or counteroffer

Our third negotiating proposal (Pricing)

Their response or counteroffer

Our second negotiating proposal (Bundling/ reconfiguration of offering)

Their response or counteroffer

Our first negotiating proposal (Timing/ invoicing)

We presented what we thought was: right plan, right bundling, right terms, right timetable—but there was some disagreement

Figure 11.1

responded to they agree with. They may simply be wait-
ing until a later point in the negotiation to bring up these
points.

Your response to their counteroffer should take into
account their objectives and propose solutions. To counter
their proposal, you can think about different ways of bundling your product, structuring payment and delivery, or
changing something about its functionality. Do *not* go to pricing immediately unless it's clear that this is the main issue for
both of you.

At each level of offer and counteroffer, the issues you're
talking about will tend to get more specific. That's because
you're finding greater and greater agreement on the underlying themes as you each discover more about what the other
wants. The scope of your talks will get narrower until you
reach that point on the pyramid when you agree and can get
to the business of drawing up and signing the deal.

There's usually no reason to rush this process; in fact, it's
much better if you don't. Try to allow some time to elapse
between when you receive a counteroffer and when you
respond to it. This does two things:

1. It gives you time to think through all the implica-
   tions of the counteroffer: what it means for the deal,
   what you can and can't live with, and what it tells you
   about your opponent's objectives and Alternative.
2. It avoids giving the impression that you're desperate
   to make a deal. If your opponent senses you're under
   time pressure, he may start to use this against you.

In general, my rule is, the bigger the deal the more time
it should take. In negotiations that are about very large

deals, try to let twenty-four hours elapse between offer and counteroffer.

SCHIFFMAN **SAYS . . .**

Your opponent makes a counteroffer very often to test the limits of what you're willing to give. He wants to find out as much as he possibly can about your Alternative and your objectives.

Sometimes there will be things he proposes that you don't want to give in on. Other points are ones on which you can make concessions. But always see the process as a two-way exchange.

Never give up something for free in a negotiation. If you make a concession, ask the other side to make one in return.

Multi-Party Negotiations

As anyone who's ever been involved in selling a house can tell you, the best situation you can be in is where two or more parties are vying simultaneously for the same thing. For sales-people, more often than not this kind of bidding war means they're competing against another party to sell the client the same product or service.

In this case, your counteroffer is going to be shaped, whether you like it or not, by whatever your competitor has bid. But—this is an important point—you don't have to follow his agenda.

Think about the following:

SALES SCENARIO

Salesperson: We can offer you 500 widgets at $1.50 per widget.

Customer: Well, I can tell you that we have another offer right now for 500 widgets at only $1.40 each. Can you do better than that?

Salesperson: Can you tell me when the other firm can deliver the widgets?

Customer: They promise three weeks.

Salesperson: And would they invoice at the time of sale or at the time of delivery?

Customer: At the time of sale.

Salesperson: Well, I can't go lower on price. But I can guarantee delivery in two weeks, and we could invoice at time of delivery, so your payment would be delayed.

Customer: Yes, I think that would work.

Just because your competitor has offered a lower price doesn't mean you have to go lower still. Remember, *price is not the thing you start with.* You have plenty of other variables you can use to structure the deal. Under the circumstances given above, it's likely that the customer will go back to your competitor with your delivery and invoicing guarantees and see if the other firm can match them. If not, you've won the sale.

The Real Deal

1. Counteroffers *must* respond to offers.
2. Use your opponent's counteroffers to learn more about her or his objectives, Alternative, and walk-away point.
3. When you're involved in multiparty negotiations, don't let your competitor set the terms of the negotiation. Find other ways of countering their offers to your customer.

CHAPTER 12

Tricks of the Trade

Some people are professional negotiators. They make their living in this arena, trading back and forth on everything from legal or financial deals to high-level political discussions. These are the people who show up on nightly news programs, having flown in from international arms negotiating sessions in Reykjavik or someplace.

As far as I know, there's no place you can go to get a college degree in negotiation. There are some classes and books, but for the most part, all these people learn how to be great negotiators by watching others do it and by practicing. And the rules for negotiating an international treaty about cod fishing rights are pretty much the same as the rules for negotiating a new contract for a client. In both instances, you have to learn a set of tactics and how to apply them.

When a negotiator starts a discussion, he has a lot of tricks at his disposal. We've talked about a few of these already, but now we're going to get into the nitty-gritty of some others. As I said in the previous chapter, at all times look for opportunities to use these in combination. They're much more powerful working together than they are separately.

Above all, be flexible. Some of the tactics you use will depend on the personality and experience of your opponent in the negotiation. In a previous chapter, I stressed the importance of having a thought-out battle plan for the session, but if you sense your tactics and strategy aren't working, come up with something new. If necessary, ask for a break in the discussions so you can rethink things and develop a new plan.

Come in Low or High

This is probably the most common tactic used by all negotiators. It comes down to this: *Always come in with something that's different from what you're willing to settle for.* You have to find a balance, of course. You don't want to come in with an offer that's insulting and marks you as unserious. But you need to give yourself some maneuvering room. Generally, I come in usually about a third below or above my final number (though it depends on the situation).

Whether you come in high or low depends, of course, on what you're negotiating. If you want to sell something to someone, come in with a unit price above the one you expect to wind up with. If you're trying to buy something, come in lower than you think you'll end up at. Especially if you're talking to someone with whom you've negotiated before, you'll develop a feel very quickly for what his range of movement is and how high or low you need to make your initial offer.

Hold Something Back

If you put all your cards on the table at the beginning of the negotiation, you've got nothing left. On the other hand, if you keep something back, you can play that card at a key moment, either when things are stalled and you need to get them going again or when you sense your opponent is vulnerable. What you have in reserve can be a small point, but it's the surprise factor that gives it value. Possibly this is something that you ruled off the table in an earlier stage of the discussion. ("I know I said we couldn't move on a minimum ship of 50,000 units, but we *might* be able to go down to 40,000.") Or possibly it's something you've not brought up before. ("Let's talk here about a product guarantee plan.")

Bluff

If you've ever played poker, you know the value of bluff. The biggest one is that you're willing to get up and walk away from the table. That can be very powerful, but it has the huge disadvantage that you can only do it once. If you use it and your opponent backs down, every time you use it after that, its value will be diminished.

But there are many smaller points on which you can bluff. Car salespeople are experienced at this sort of thing. I don't know how many times you've bought a car and bargained with the salesperson about the price, but I can virtually guarantee you that on every one of those occasions the salesperson said, "Let me go into the back and discuss this with my manager." That's a bluff; they're presenting you with a fake authority figure to make you back down on your demand. It's possible that the salesperson really does talk to his manager, but he's already made a decision about how to counter your offer.

Silence

Salespeople (and other negotiators) don't make use of this tactic nearly as often as they should. Silence can be your friend. In some of my other books, I've mentioned the axiom, "Set it up, and then shut up!" The point is that too often in the midst of the sale, the salesperson keeps talking and gives away information she or he doesn't need to.

In negotiations, silence puts pressure on the other party to respond. You'll find that when you're silent, sooner or later the other person will start talking. Maybe nature abhors silence. I don't know. But the fact is that by keeping your mouth shut, you'll force the other person to talk. And then they'll be the one giving away information, which you can use as the negotiation proceeds.

Use Time Wisely

I absolutely hate being late. When I'm coming close to running late, my hands start to sweat, my stomach clenches up, and I start looking at my watch every ten seconds or so. Many people are similarly sensitive to time. In a negotiation, this is a powerful tool you can use to your advantage.

Watch the time, and watch how your opponent reacts to it. If you get the feeling that he's worried about running late, that may be a good time to increase the intensity of the negotiation. At the same time, you don't want the most important elements of the negotiation to be settled in the last three minutes. Keep in mind that when you're negotiating a sale, *it's always easier for the client to say no than yes.* Don't help her to say no by trying to cram the main negotiating point into the end of the session.

Good Cop/Bad Cop

Anyone who's ever watched a cop show on television is familiar with this one. Still, clichéd as it is, it can work.

The bad cop doesn't even have to be in the room. When you're faced with something you want to turn down, just say, for example, "Well, gosh, I'd like to give you some flex room there, but my boss won't let me. She's said we have to be absolutely rigid regarding our payment schedules. If it were up to me, I'd be happy to accommodate you, but she's the one who makes those decisions."

If the person playing bad cop is in the room with you, I recommend she stay very silent. As I said, silence can be very intimidating.

Anger and Happiness

I mentioned a couple of chapters ago that it's key in a successful negotiation to remain in control of your emotions. That isn't to say you can't display any. In fact, if you go through the whole session acting like an automaton, chances are whomever you're talking to is going to be turned off. At a minimum, he'll think you're pretty weird.

Anger is a good tool to use in a negotiation as long as you control it rather than letting it control you. Just keep in mind that no one ever won the deal by punching the other guy in the face. It sounds stupid, but it's true.

I was once involved in a negotiation conducted by phone with a salesperson, someone I didn't know at all. I listened to his pitch, and then we began to discuss terms. I must have pushed his buttons in some way, because I could sense as our conversation went on that he was getting angrier and angrier. I tried everything I could think of to calm him down and get us back on track, but nothing seemed to work. Finally he burst out, "I just don't think you have any respect for me as a person or as a salesman!" I heard a loud "click" on the other end of the line as he slammed down the phone.

Needless to say, I never heard from him again, and I didn't make any attempt to contact him or his company. If he got that genuinely angry during a phone call, what kind of service could I expect from him? He didn't punch me in the face, but he might as well have with that attitude.

On the other hand, happiness can work for you as well. I believe there's a part of us that likes to make other people happy. If you act pleased when you win something in the negotiation, your client may be inclined to do other things to please you.

SCHIFFMAN **SAYS . . .**

Part of the art of negotiating is learning to read the other person. This applies not only to her or his words, but also to body language, dress, and so on. If you sense that something you've said is making your opponent nervous or unhappy, note it down.

Take mental notes throughout the negotiation. If you don't use the information now, you may later.

The Real Deal

1. Tactics are better used in combination than separately.
2. Adapt your tactics to the situation and personalities you're dealing with. Don't be rigid and stick to a preconceived plan despite evidence that it isn't working.
3. Emotions such as happiness and anger are useful tools in a negotiation as long as they're controlled. Untrammeled rage in a negotiation isn't likely to damage anyone but you.

CHAPTER 13

What *Not* to Do

It's a sad fact, but negotiations are blown all the time. As I hope you appreciate by this point in the book, negotiations are tricky, complicated things, and it doesn't take much to gum up the works—sometimes beyond any repair.

SALES SCENARIO

I was talking to a Realtor recently about house sales and asked if there were cases of sales blowing up during the final closing, the meeting at which everyone sits in a lawyer's office and signs the papers and turns over the keys. She said that yes, it had happened just recently to a deal she was brokering.

The parties had done a lot of close negotiating during the months leading up to the sale. There had been a lot of conflict (stimulated by the fact that the housing market, at the time, wasn't very good), and all sides were tense.

While the two families were sitting in the room for the final closing, some minor point arose. An argument started, tempers flared, and before five minutes had passed, the buyers were banging on the table, while the sellers were standing up and shouting. Before the real estate brokers could calm the situation, both sides had stalked out, leaving the papers in the sale unsigned. Months of patient work by all sorts of people went down the tubes because both parties involved started acting like children.

In this chapter, we'll look at some of the things you should avoid during a negotiation. Fortunately, most of them are a matter of common sense.

Most of the time, when a negotiation breaks down, it's not difficult to get it back on track. Sometimes it's a simple matter of both parties taking a few hours, days, or weeks to cool off and get a more rational perspective on the discussion. But if you avoid the mistakes I discuss in this chapter, you'll minimize the chance of the negotiation going off track.

Words to Avoid

When I was a little kid—and quite possibly when you were a child—I had occasion to repeat the rhyme:

Sticks and stones will break my bones,
But names can never hurt me.

Sadly, as I grew older I realized this isn't true. Names *can* hurt. Words can injure. And in a negotiation, which is made up of people talking to one another, words have a lot of power, some good, some bad.

In negotiation, there are some words you should generally avoid. Sometimes you'll find yourself using them, but mostly they're good words to keep away from.

never
always
dishonest
untrue
liar
stupid
silly
can't
won't

Don't Get Personal

One of the most important things to keep in mind about any negotiation is *it's not about you.* The discussions you're involved in have nothing to do with how you and your opponent feel about each other, about your ego, your reputation, or your integrity. They're about the issues on the table that are being discussed. It's essential that you separate yourself from those issues. This may be difficult because you probably feel quite passionately about some of them. I said at the very beginning of this book that to be an effective negotiator you have to believe in yourself and in what you're negotiating about. And I still stand by that. But you can't lose sight of the bigger issue. *What is your main objective? What do you mean by winning?*

If you make the negotiations solely about you and your ego, it changes the answer to those two questions. And when you do that, you lose track of what's best for your organization.

Of course, your opponent may very well be trying to make you think it's all about you. He may be saying, implicitly or explicitly, that if you can't successfully complete this negotiation you're inferior to him. If you notice this happening, take a step back. Your opponent is trying to control the negotiations. It's time for you to reassert control.

Don't Lie

I've already given my opinion about lying during negotiations, so I'll just reiterate it here. Lying is counterproductive. It ruins your relationships with business clients, traps you in an ever-growing web of deceit, and sooner or later it catches up with you. Just ask Bernard Madoff.

It *is* permissible to do some creative exaggeration. For example, you may find it expedient to suggest that something is a bigger concession than it really is or that the price of something is really low when in fact, from your point of view, it's quite reasonable. But outright lying is going to get you in a lot of hot water.

If you suspect the person on the other side of the table is lying, it's best not to accuse him outright. You can try to find a polite way of contradicting him by reference to a neutral source of information. For example:

Customer: I know it's a high order, but I don't anticipate any significant returns. We're seeing a growth in the number of our stores just now.

You: Really? That's interesting, because there was a report in the *Wall Street Journal* last week that eight of the branches have closed and two more are downsizing significantly. With that in mind, do you think we should lower this order a bit?

Or would you prefer to guarantee a larger number of units as nonreturnable?

Notice that in this exchange you're not using any highly charged words ("liar," "wrong"), but are relying on the very neutral word "interesting" to express your disbelief in the customer's statement.

Don't Slam Doors

Obviously this is true in a literal sense—unless you have calculated that a dramatic exit from the room is what's required to get the negotiation going down the right path. But I'm also thinking of this in its metaphorical sense.

SCHIFFMAN **SAYS . . .**

Having at one point been through a particularly bitter discussion, I couldn't resist telling the other person, "I'm really glad I'll never have to see or speak to you again." The world of sales professionals being small, of course, I did see him again, and my angry remark cost me some valuable contacts.

Whether you win or lose the negotiation, maintain the relationship. You never know what may come out of it.

Once I was involved in a negotiation in which the other party won. She had more of an edge than I could get, and she got more from me than I wanted to give. She made a big deal of rubbing it in, trying to denigrate me and the work I'd done. Five years later I returned to the company and this time I won everything I'd come for. She was also present at those negotiations, but her role had been downgraded to assisting in handing out the materials.

I'd like to think it was karma, since I believe that what goes around comes around. But I also believe it was the logical result of her tendency to grind down anyone she'd beaten in a negotiation. You don't make a lot of friends that way, and sooner or later the people you've tried to humiliate will strike back at you.

Don't Dismiss Your Opponent's Viewpoint

I suppose this bit of advice might be labeled Try to Think the Best of People.

Assume, until you have reason to think otherwise, that the person with whom you're negotiating is sincere and honest. Start from the premise that they believe, as you do, in the position they're defending. To belittle them or make fun of them is, first of all, incredibly rude and disrespectful, and second it's counterproductive. It makes you seem like a bully, someone other people won't want to do business with.

A friend of mine once negotiated with a businessman who, after they had signed the deal, explained in detail all the things my friend had done wrong and what a better deal he could have gotten if he'd pushed harder on some points. I wasn't there, of course, and for all I know my friend probably *could* have made a better deal. The point is it was out of line for his opponent to tell him so.

Not surprisingly, my friend recommended to his company that they not do business with this guy again. His arrogance and self-satisfaction cost him a valuable commission.

Just remember: It's not about you. It's about winning.

The Real Deal

1. When you're negotiating, avoid charged words and phrases that can escalate an argument.
2. Don't call into question your opponent's integrity or intelligence.
3. Remember that nothing lasts forever. Wherever possible, avoid closing doors on the other party; leave open the possibility of resuming negotiations at a future point, either on this or some other deal.

CHAPTER 14

Who Are You Talking To?

I'm sure most of you are familiar with Robert Louis Stevenson's great story "The Strange Case of Dr. Jekyll and Mr. Hyde." Even if you've never read it, you may have seen the movie, starring Spencer Tracy and Ingrid Bergman. In any case, you probably know the story of the kind Dr. Jekyll who, upon drinking a mysterious potion, transforms into the cruel, murderous Mr. Hyde.

My point is that for some people, negotiation acts a bit like that potion. They're pleasant, easygoing, intelligent. Then they get involved in a negotiation, and a completely different side to their personality comes to the fore. On the other hand, there are people who can sit at a negotiating table and remain as calm and patient as they are in ordinary life.

In this chapter, I want to look at what kinds of personalities you'll commonly encounter in negotiations. Some of them are easy to deal with. Others can be a pain in the neck. But based on my experience over the years, I have some suggestions for how to get around the personality issues and keep the negotiation going in a fruitful direction. At the outset of this, though, I ask you to keep in mind the Jekyll-Hyde contrast I just mentioned. Just because someone's nice outside the boardroom doesn't mean she or he is going to stay that way when you're bargaining with them.

Aggressive

This is one of the easiest negotiating types to recognize and one of the most common. Many people confuse being effective in debate with being loud and angry. As I've said before, there's a place in negotiation for controlled anger (and there's a time and a place to raise your voice), but the key is the word "controlled."

Aggressive negotiators, on the other hand, sometimes don't seem to have any control. From the beginning of the discussion, they're loud, and they push every position and every demand as if their life depended on it.

Even their body language is a giveaway. They sit on the edge of their seats, lean forward across the table, and make broad, sweeping gestures. Their voices are pitched a bit louder than necessary, so that not only can you hear them but most of the foot traffic passing the conference room gets the benefit of their wisdom as well. Often when you speak, they'll act dismissive, leaning back in their chairs, looking away, ostentatiously checking their BlackBerry.

There's a lot of room in negotiation for aggressive behavior—after all, I've been comparing a negotiation to combat—but there's a fine line between controlled aggressive behavior as a tactic and bullying.

If you're facing someone who's overly aggressive, don't be afraid to push back. Most bullies collapse when confronted with strength. You need to assert yourself and make it clear that you won't be railroaded into a bad deal. If necessary, exercise your option to walk. Believe me, I've done it before.

Passive

Just as problematic as the bullying client is the one who doesn't seem to have much interest in the negotiation. He sits there, like a lump on a log, not saying much, not offering any solutions or reactions.

SCHIFFMAN SAYS . . .

I've recommended over and over again that you ask lots of questions. But some kinds of questions are better than others. Don't ask questions that can be answered with a simple "yes" or "no." You want to get your clients talking.

Always ask open-ended questions that have to be answered in full sentences and paragraphs.

In some cases, it's because he's lost interest in the company and is on his way out. If you establish that this is the case, I'd recommend suspending the negotiation until you can talk to someone who's going to be more invested in it. An executive who's preparing his exit from the company isn't going to be able to do you or your product any good.

However, in some cases, that's his style. He doesn't say much and lets others do the talking. The trick, then, is to get him to enter the discussion.

With people like this, there's no substitute for asking more questions. It gets them talking and contributes to your store of information. If they don't want to talk, try throwing out outrageous suggestions or statements—always making it clear that you're doing so in a humorous vein. At least they'll be forced to respond when you suggest that rather than getting a discount from you for bulk orders, they should increase their unit price on all orders over 5,000.

Uncooperative

Again, you have to try to separate out when someone's using noncooperation as a negotiating tactic and when that's just part of who they are.

A couple of years ago, I was in a series of discussions with a woman who had the most downer personality I've ever come across. Even when I said "Hi" to her, she looked as if the bottom had fallen out of her world. She walked about the office with her head down, shoulders hunched, glaring at the floor as if it owed her an apology. Anything I proposed she was against. Whenever I made a suggestion, she'd heave a great sigh, roll her eyes, and explain why it couldn't be done.

The danger of people like that is that they can draw you into their pessimistic world-view. Before you know it, you start accepting all the limitations they propose, and the negotiation bogs down or collapses. After all, who wants to put together a deal that's so obviously doomed to fail?

In the case of this woman, I had to pull myself together and try to find some way of re-energizing our discussion. I tried several different tactics, but none of them worked. Finally, in desperation one day I started asking her some questions about what she did outside of work for fun.

It turns out that she was an enthusiastic amateur sailor. She and her husband owned a boat and spent most weekends on it, either sailing or doing repairs and maintenance. Now, I don't know a spliced jib from a boom, but I showed interest in what she was telling me. Soon she was sitting up, her eyes sparkling, laughing and joking as she told me about some of their recent nautical adventures. The more I asked about it, the more animated she became.

Finally, after a half hour or so of this conversation, none of which had the remotest connection to the subject of our negotiation, we picked up where we'd left off. But what a difference! The energy she'd felt when we talked about sailing still infused her, and she interacted with me in an overwhelmingly positive manner. We found a couple of simple solutions to points we'd been stuck on, and I wound up the deal in a way very favorable to me.

The lesson: Sometimes you have to go outside the context of the business relationship to find out what makes people tick. I believe that everyone has some kind of passion; some people have lots of them. Everyone feels strongly about something. If you can find out what that something is and get them talking about it, you'll be amazed at how quickly they shake off their indifference and lassitude. When that happens, you know you've turned things around.

The Real Deal

1. Determine the personality type you're negotiating with to figure out how to get the most out of your discussions.
2. Ask open-ended questions to get the most information from your client.
3. Don't be afraid to ask questions that extend beyond the business relationship in order to find out what makes your opponent tick.

CHAPTER 15

What to Do When
the Discussion Stalls

One way to look at a negotiation is as if it's a play. An opening act sets up the problem, followed by a middle section in which the characters discuss the problem, and then a final act in which the characters arrive at a solution.

A while ago, I went to a play in New York, where I live. It wasn't a play I was familiar with, so I didn't know what to expect. Throughout the first act, I followed the plot with interest. But as we got into the second act, I found myself yawning and surreptitiously glancing at my watch. Around me, I could feel other members of the audience doing the same thing.

The audience restlessness seemed to communicate itself to the actors, and their performances turned lackluster. The second half of the drama was excruciating. After it was over and the curtain had mercifully fallen, most of the audience headed to the nearest bar. I walked away from the theater vowing never again to watch a play by that author. For that matter, I avoided that theater for a long time. I may even have subconsciously resisted walking down that street.

My point? A badly written play is like a bad negotiation. It pulls the energy out of everyone and, if it goes very bad, can permanently damage the relationship between you and your client.

If you find yourself in a negotiation that's stalling, there are several things you can do to breathe life back into it:

- Redefine the problem
- Redefine the solution
- Ask more questions

Redefining the Problem

Sometimes despite all the goodwill in the world, a negotiation reaches an impasse. Neither side can seem to break out of their positions, and you find yourself returning to the same points over and over again.

When that happens, you need to ask yourself, "Are we negotiating over the right issue?"

This may take a radical reorganization of your thinking, and there are some exercises you can do to break your mind free of the trap it's in. If you can stop the discussion for a while, go somewhere quiet and sit. Let your mind wander. You need to get into a peaceful frame of mind. When you're relaxed, take out a pen and a piece of paper. Make a list of what you think are the major issues you're talking about, starting with the most important. Then go down the list and ask yourself after each one, "What happens if I don't get it? What happens if I don't win?"

On that list, there should be one issue that all the others depend on. That's the deal breaker, the point the whole negotiation hinges on. The question is, is that what you've been talking about all this time?

Too many times, I've seen negotiations get hung up on silly points that draw everything else after them. These points are like vacuums; when they come up, all of a sudden all the energy and goodwill that's been built up drains away, and you're left with nothing but irritation and outright anger. Often when that happens, it's a sign that what you're talking about isn't necessarily that important. (Political science professor Wallace Sayle once famously observed that the reason academic disputes are so vicious is because the stakes are so small.)

Redefining the Solution

It's possible that both you and your opponent have defined winning in a way that makes it impossible for either of you to really win.

For example, a sales rep I know was once involved in trying to negotiate a sale to a small company in the Midwest. The buyer was adamant that they had to have the product in ten days. The rep was equally firm that a ten-day delivery time would result in a 150 percent increase in the price. The company rep said that he had no authority to negotiate a higher price and couldn't get that past his bosses. The discussion went on for two weeks by phone and e-mail until eventually the sales rep realized he was wasting his time and broke off the deal.

Of course, you could argue that this ought to have been foreseen from the very beginning of the negotiation once both sides made their positions clear. But remember that a negotiation is a dialogue. As such, it's an evolving, changing animal. It can take that back and forth exchange between you and your client to reveal just how opposed your positions are.

When that happens, sometimes there's nothing for it but to walk away. I'll deal with this in depth in an upcoming chapter. But before you give up on winning the sale, ask yourself if there's some other way you can define the solution. That is, what's another way for you to win?

This might mean settling for less than you originally wanted. As I've said before, I think it's better to walk away with a piece of a deal than with no deal at all. But it also might mean getting something unexpected out of the deal that you hadn't thought of before.

SALES SCENARIO

Salesperson: What I'm proposing here is that you take delivery of 10,000 units at the end of July for a unit price of $5.50.

Customer: No. That's not going to work. I've told you before. We can only take 5,000 units, and we're not going above $4 a unit. That's what I'm sticking to, and I don't know why you don't just accept that.

Salesperson: Well, let's think about this. How important is the unit cost to you?

Customer: Very important.

Salesperson: More important than the delivery date?

Customer: Yes.

Salesperson: More important than how many units you take?

> **Customer:** Well, maybe. They're both important.
>
> **Salesperson:** Is your main concern with the warehousing costs?
>
> **Customer:** That's right.
>
> **Salesperson:** Well, how about this? You take delivery of 7,500 units at the end of July. Then you take the balance of 10,000, which would be 2,500 units, in November. You're saving warehousing costs on that.
>
> **Customer:** That might work. What unit price?
>
> **Salesperson:** Well, since you're not taking 10,000 units immediately, how about if we set the unit price at $4 per unit for the first 5,000 units and $5.50 a unit for the rest.
>
> **Customer:** Okay. I can go with that.

In the above example, rather than allowing both parties to remain locked in conflicting positions, you were able to figure out an arrangement that redefined the terms of the sale. In other words, you redefined what it meant to win. In doing so, you made the customer also redefine winning, and the whole thing worked out to your mutual benefit.

Ask Questions

To either redefine the problem or redefine the solution, you need to do the third thing on our list: Ask questions. This is basic to breaking any stalemate, because additional information acts as a lubricant to get the parts of the deal-making process working again.

Don't assume that because you're involved in the actual negotiation that the time for asking questions has expired. You should continue to accumulate facts throughout the process. Whatever doesn't immediately play a part in your discussions, you can put in the bank for future negotiations with the customer.

In the previous example, notice that the salesperson is trying to find out more about the client's priorities—what matters most in the deal. The more you know about that, the easier it is to arrive at a successful conclusion. Because you can figure out more accurately how your interests and those of your client can come together.

The Real Deal

1. If a negotiation stalls, try redefining the problem or redefining the solution.
2. If you can't agree on a point, try to find something else on which you can come to agreement and then come back to the original issue.
3. The more information you have, the easier it will be to break a stalemate.

CHAPTER 16

When to Be Tough, and When to Be Easy

Any book on negotiation techniques sooner or later has to include a story about buying a used car.

There's a good reason for this: In America we've largely given up the tradition of haggling over price. When we go for a quart of milk, we don't stand at the checkout counter dickering with the clerk about how much we're going to pay for it. The clerk swipes the milk over the bar code reader, the register dings, and the price comes up on the screen.

And that's the price we pay. We've been acclimated to this idea that commodities have a fixed price, and everybody (well, everybody who shops at that store) pays the same thing for a quart of milk.

This is true of almost every purchase we make during our lives. But there are two big exceptions, and interestingly they're for two of the biggest purchases we'll ever make. One is our house. The other is our car.

Driven By a Little Old Lady

A couple of years ago, I was in a bad auto accident. A couple of kids in an SUV slammed into my car mid-intersection and smashed it into a fence. My car was totaled—ironically, the SUV was barely damaged.

A couple of weeks after the accident, I got a check from the insurance company for $5,000 to cover the cost of my car. As it happens, I didn't want to spend more than $5,000 on another car, so that was fine with me. I went to a dealership, and a nice young man approached me. I explained I was in the market for a used car and wanted to spend no more than $5,000.

Then it started.

"Well, I've got a great car over here that I could let you have for $6,300," he said.

"But I only want to spend $5,000," I countered.

"Well, over here is a car that's a bargain at $5,899. Plus tax, of course."

"No. I only want to spend $5,000," I repeated. I could feel the sweat of irritation breaking out under my collar.

He sighed and took me to another car. "*This* one," he announced grandly, "is only $5,200 plus tax. A bargain. It's—"

I lifted my hand and stopped him mid-sentence.

"No. I said I *only want to spend $5,000.* That's *all* I'm going to spend. That's everything. Price. Tax. Everything."

There was a long pause while we both looked at each other. Then he said, "Okay. Come this way."

We went into the backroom, and he showed me another car. "This one," he said, "is ten years old. But it's only got 35,000 miles on it. It was—" I swear this is what he said— "driven by a little old lady who only went to church and the grocery store."

"How much?" I asked.

"Well, with tax, that would come out to $5,150."

105

I shook my head, turned around, and started to walk away. Behind me, I could feel him sighing again. Then he said, "All right. $5,000."

That was the car I bought. For $5,000. Not a penny more.

As far as car negotiations go, this one is a bit atypical, because I wouldn't compromise. I came in knowing what I wanted to spend, and ultimately that's what I spent. But I'm telling it here precisely to show you that there are times when not compromising pays off.

The salesman played a classic negotiating card right at the beginning. He came in high on the first car he showed me, obviously expecting that I'd counter with a lower price and we'd meet somewhere in the middle. It just so happens that I'd made up my mind before even walking onto the lot that I wasn't going to do that.

Now, if you take that approach to every negotiation you're involved in, you'll never get anywhere. Part of your ability to be a successful bargainer has to be your talent for compromise. But every now and then, what you need to win means the other party coming to your position. Not partly but entirely.

Back to the Alternative

Some of this goes back to the concept of the best Alternative to a Deal, which I talked about in Chapter 8. In the case of my car purchase, I knew that if this guy didn't eventually show me a car that I could buy for $5,000, there were plenty of other car dealerships around. The street I was on was lousy with them. So I knew, and he knew, I had a lot of alternatives. I could afford to hang tough and not compromise.

I'm not clairvoyant, but I can give a fair representation of what the salesperson who sold me the car was thinking. A voice in his head was probably saying, "This guy is sticking to his price, so he's either already got a car he's seen at another dealer for under $5,000, or he's confident he can find one. I have to make my commission this month, so I really want to sell him a car. At $5,000, I'm still making money, so I can do the deal. If I keep pushing, he may walk away, and I won't have anything."

Things would have been different if I'd been making the deal in a small town (I wasn't) with only one car dealership. Then there would have been a lot more pressure on me because I wouldn't have had many alternatives. I probably would have wound up paying in excess of the price I wanted. I wouldn't have been happy about it, but I might not have had much choice, assuming I really needed a car.

SCHIFFMAN **SAYS . . .**

The easiest time to be tough in a negotiation is when you have an alternative and your opponent knows you have one. You have a psychological advantage because you know you can walk away.

If you want to be tough in a negotiation, be sure you've
got a strong Alternative to fall back on.

When to Be Easy

The other side, of course, is that there are times when you'll show a lot of flexibility. This doesn't have to be a sign of weakness; in fact, it shouldn't be. Instead, it's a valuable tactic.

NEGOTIATION TECHNIQUES *(That Really Work!)*

SALES SCENARIO

Customer: I need 3,000 units by next Monday. How about if we say forty-three cents a unit?
Salesperson: That's a bit less than I was thinking.
Customer: Sorry. That's my bottom line.
Salesperson: Well, I'll tell you what. Your business is important to me, so I'm willing to go to forty-three cents for this deal. I'll have to call my office and confirm that we can do it for that, but I'm sure I can persuade them.
Customer: Thanks. I really appreciate that.
Salesperson: No problem. As I said, we value you as a customer, and we want to keep you happy. At the same time, I have to say that next Monday is tight. Could we go to next Thursday instead?
Customer: Yes, that'd work.

Notice that the salesperson in this scenario emphasizes that the relationship with the customer is valuable to him. If he's done his homework, he's calculated a monetary value for that relationship and factored it into his Alternative, so he knows, for this deal at least, he can accept a forty-three-cent price per unit. At the same time, he preserves one of my cardinal rules in any negotiation: *He doesn't give away something for nothing.* He uses the goodwill generated by being easy on the price to get a better delivery date.

You can be easy in a negotiation on a point that's less important to you, one that won't affect the main goals you've set for yourself as the outcome of the bargaining. And that willingness to accommodate your client can come back to you in the form of concessions the client is willing to give in return.

The Real Deal

1. The best time not to compromise is when you have a strong fallback position.
2. Concessions are a useful tool in any negotiation, helping to strengthen a relationship with the customer and spurring him to compromise on other points.
3. Even when making a concession, don't give away something for nothing.

CHAPTER 17

Calling It Quits

Sometimes you just get to the end of your rope. Maybe your opponent has pushed your buttons and you can't stand it any more. Maybe you realize that the negotiation has stalled and nothing you've done has moved it off Stop. Whatever the reason, it's over.

A year or so back, I was negotiating a deal with someone I'd never worked with before. It wasn't tremendously important, but as our discussion went on, I found myself getting angry and aggressive and putting more emotional energy into the negotiation than was warranted.

I took a couple of breaks to calm down, but every time I went back into the room, the same thing happened. The more rational part of my brain finally kicked in and told me that this guy was making every effort to push me into a corner. Every time I tried to find a solution that worked for me, he'd cut me off. Every time I suggested a new way of looking at it, he'd dismiss it.

Finally, I pushed back my chair and stood up. "This is going nowhere!" I said. "We're done." And I walked out. I didn't slam the door behind me, but I thought about it.

In the situation I've just described, I was mad—something that happens to me a lot, but I've learned to control it. I reacted emotionally to the situation. But in looking back on it, I still think I was right to walk out.

I probably could have stayed in the room and, with a lot of effort and heartburn, hammered out a deal. But it was clear this wasn't going to be a productive relationship, and I knew that if I had to go through this kind of agony every time I talked to this guy, I was going to get an ulcer.

When to Walk Out When You Don't Mean It

You don't always walk out in anger. Not real anger, anyway. Paradoxically, there are times when walking out of a negotiation session is the only way to get it moving.

It's a little bit like dealing with a recalcitrant puppy who's determined to roll around in some smelly patch of God-knows-what, no matter how many times you tell him no. At a certain point, a gentle wap on the butt with a rolled-up newspaper will at least get his attention. And that's what threatening to walk out of a negotiation will do: get somebody's attention.

SALES SCENARIO

Customer: I've told you before that we're not going to take more than fifty units. And there's no way you're getting away with that price! I know what you're trying to do. You're high-balling me. Are you just trying to prove something?

Salesperson: I think you misunderstand. There's been a—
Customer: I don't want to hear it! The price is out of the question, and you'd better come up with something else!
Salesperson: Okay. Clearly, we're not going to get anywhere if you question my integrity. We need to negotiate in good faith, and you've used up all of mine. Contact my office if you want to talk some more. Otherwise, we're all done.

In this example, if the situation is allowed to continue as it does at the opening, things are going to get worse. The customer isn't listening, isn't in a mood to give and take. The salesperson has to do something to break the pattern. So she tells the customer what the problem is that he's creating (questioning integrity); tells him how to fix it (negotiate in good faith); and tells him what to do if he wants to start the negotiation again (call the office).

The very fact that the salesperson has left direction to call her office tells us that she expects negotiations to continue. She may get all the way to the door before the customer asks her to come back and sit down. Or she may go through the door and go back to her office before he calls. But in most cases, he'll call, and things can get started again on a more productive note.

How do you know if you can walk out of a negotiation and still leave room for it to resume? Your research and your Alternative and *especially* your estimate of your opponent's Alternative should give you a lot of clues. Ask yourself: Can my client afford not to do this deal? What happens to him if it falls through? If he has to come to an agreement with you, walking out can be a powerful tool.

However—and I can't stress this enough—it's a tool you can *only use once* during a negotiation. If, every time you get to a hard place in the talks, you jump up and shout, "I'm leaving!" no one will take you seriously. The other party must believe that you're ready and willing to walk out of the negotiation rather than let them continue down the path they're taking.

SCHIFFMAN **SAYS . . .**

Sometimes in a negotiation, you'll find that the discussion escalates not only in the issues being discussed, but also in the tone and pace of the conversation. When your opponent is getting angry, he'll tend to speak louder and faster. You need to change the pace of the exchange.

If your opponent is talking louder, speak softer. If she's talking faster, slow down your speech.

When to Walk Out If You Do Mean It

I know it's difficult, but it's always better in a negotiation to let your head rule your heart.

Think of it like a boxing match. When you're dancing around the ring, throwing jabs and uppercuts, you're trying to think through your strategy, everything your coach told you, thinking about your next move and about the other fighter's moves.

Then his fist shoots out and knocks you back a foot, and all of a sudden your strategy goes out the window.

That's how fights are lost. The boxer is staggered by a sudden blow to the head or the body, and while he's reeling, without anything in his mind but staying upright, he's vulnerable. His opponent slams into him with slashing fists, and before you know it, the referee has thrown in the towel, signaling that the fight is over.

Fights are won when, despite repeated blows, the boxer keeps his cool and remembers what he's doing. He can continue to look for openings, and sooner or later he finds one and exploits it. The great Muhammad Ali was like that. He was a crafty fighter who rarely lost his temper in the ring. That's why he was "The Greatest."

What does this have to do with walking out during a negotiation? Just this: Walking out should be a rational, not an emotional response. You should walk away from a negotiation and mean it for any one of the following reasons:

- The deal has no chance of being made. Shake hands, say, "Thanks for your time. I'm sorry we couldn't come to an agreement," and walk out.
- The negotiation has evolved to the point that if the deal is made it will be bad for you. Again, shake hands and end the discussion amicably.
- The deal could still be made, but the cost to you in terms of emotional capital is too great. This can happen if your client isn't treating you respectfully or is being abusive. Resist the temptation to put on a big scene. Just smile, tell him you're done, and walk out. Don't waste words, but make it clear there's no room for reopening the discussion.

Yelling and door slamming don't do much when you're walking away from a deal. In fact, to anyone watching, it can look childish. If you really feel like that, go home and punch a pillow for a while. Or go somewhere by yourself and rant and rave to the air. You'll feel better afterward.

But remember that at some point in the future you and your opponent may be back at the conference table with something important at stake. So as much as possible, don't break off relations, and try to end on a civil note.

The Real Deal

1. Threatening to walk out of a negotiation can get your opponent's attention and jump-start the discussion,

2. You can only threaten to walk out once during a negotiation.

3. Walk away from a negotiation if there's no chance of the deal being made or if it will be a bad deal for you.

CHAPTER 18

The End Game

Every chess game is divided into the opening, the middle game, and the end game. In the opening, both sides are maneuvering for position, usually to try to control the middle of the board. In the middle game, they're struggling to expand their control of space and to win material from one another.

In the end game, the board has been cleared of irrelevant pieces. Now the game comes down to the movement of just a few very powerful pieces trying to checkmate one another's king.

Negotiations are, as I've said earlier, a lot like chess, with this significant difference: In a chess game, there's room for only one winner. No Grand Master has ever looked across the board at his opponent and said, "Let's find a solution that works for both of us."

In any negotiation, there can be winners and losers. And there can be two winners and no losers. The best bargainers strive to find a deal in which both sides will be able to claim victory. Nonetheless, the reality is that you want to win. And in the latter stages of the negotiation you may find yourself pushing very hard to close the deal and get the best possible terms for yourself. Your opponent is doing the same thing. Each of you is striving to checkmate the other.

The Negotiation "Middle Game"

The first part of the game is all about positioning. In chess, both players are trying, in their opening moves, to control the center of the board. In the same way, when you open a negotiation, you and your opponent are both trying to move into the center of the discussion and control it. Remember: the more you control the negotiation, the better a deal you're going to get out of it.

Once you've established the rhythm and flow of your exchanges with your opponent, you move into the middle game. In chess, an important function of the middle game is to "develop" the major pieces, such as bishops, knights, rooks, and the queen (in chess parlance, "develop" means to get those pieces off the back row and toward the center of the board where they can do something).

Similarly, in a negotiation, the point of the middle game is to muster your major arguments and get them busy. This is where you and your client will use your knowledge of one another's objectives to try to gain an advantage. You can evaluate the strength of her arguments and find talking points.

A second point of the middle game is to clear the board of extraneous material. This allows players to see more clearly where the lines of strength, attack, and defense are on the board.

In your negotiation, you want to push away the unimportant issues and figure out the major points to be decided. Sometimes those smaller things can clutter up a negotiation and take valuable time away from arriving at an agreement.

This is where you can find out what your opponent's *real* objective is. I've stressed the importance of understanding what the person on the other side of the table wants from the negotiation. But just because it's important, don't think she or he's going to tell you. The fact of the matter is, they may not entirely know themselves.

SCHIFFMAN **SAYS** . . .

Sometimes your client doesn't want to talk about his real objectives in the relatively formal setting of a negotiation, but he's willing to tell you what they are in a more relaxed atmosphere. If you sense that he's holding out on you, try going off the record.

Have sidebar discussions with your opponents in settings other than the negotiations themselves, in order to understand their objectives, the pressures on them, and their Alternatives.

A while ago, I decided to shut down my company, DEI. It was a difficult decision, since I'd run the company for a number of years, but I felt it was the right thing to do. It caused some consternation among my clients, both past and present. One guy called me up and told me that since DEI was shutting down, I had an obligation to refund some money he'd paid for training.

We went back and forth on it for a little while, and I finally told him I wasn't going to refund the money.

He said, "Well, then can I have a job?"

That was his real objective. The money was a means of getting there. What he wanted, in fact, was a regular paycheck.

Why didn't he just tell me this at the outset? It's hard to say. But people very often don't reveal their regular agendas. It's part of your job to make them come to you.

Winning the End Game

Once the middle game stage is over, you're ready to move into the end game. In chess, this is sometimes played with very few pieces on the board. Yet it's one of the most dynamic and exciting parts of the game.

In a negotiation, this is where you need to go to a full court press to get what you want from the bargaining. It's also where the other side is turning up the pressure, so you need to be at your most alert.

A friend of mine told me about a complicated negotiation he was recently involved in. The talks went on for weeks, involving anywhere from five and twenty people on each side. There were dozens of issues that they batted back and forth, hauling in their legal staffs at every stage to vet the agreements they were hammering out.

Finally, they got down to the last day of the discussions. My friend's boss was conducting the negotiations for his company. Everyone was tired, but they were satisfied that they'd worked out the best deal possible. The only people sitting in the room were the top leaders of both companies and their immediate aides.

The executive—the one my friend worked for—leaned forward and said to everyone at the table, "All right, now we'll get to the important stuff. Just what kind of a relationship are we going to have for the next five years?"

There was a painful silence for a few minutes. You could see everyone beginning to roll their eyes ("What's the *matter* with this guy? Doesn't he know we've been talking about this stuff for days?").

Then an exec on the other side nodded and said, "Yes, I know what you mean. We've got all the detailed stuff out of the way, so let's talk about the big issues."

The funny thing was, the discussions they'd had about the small stuff paved the way for a quick, strong agreement on the big issue of their business relationship. Everyone walked away from the table with a renewed sense of energy and purpose.

The end game in negotiation is among the most important parts of the discussion. That goes double when the talks have been long and hard. At this juncture, there are several tactics you can use to turn up the heat.

- **Focus on time.** Say, "I've got to resolve this issue by 5 P.M. That's when my boss will be calling me, and I need a decision by then." This gives your opponent a definite timeline for the discussion. The drawback is you can only use it once. A deadline that's continually extended loses any force.

- **Argue for a comprehensive solution.** Even though I've said before that I prefer a partial deal over no deal, there's a lot to be said for demanding that your opponent reach agreement on *all* the points. This pressures him to look beyond a nickel-and-dime solution to one that may contain some important concessions.

- **Fortify your position.** The harder your opponent pushes at this stage, the more you stand pat. Imply that there's just no room for compromise. Remember, at this stage you're negotiating about things that are fundamental, so any concession either of you makes will be magnified in importance.

- **Escalate your tone.** You don't have to be nasty, but there's nothing wrong with ramping up your assertiveness. The end game of a negotiation is a good time to make clear what you will and won't give in on.
- **Emphasize the consequences of not reaching a deal.** If you know his Alternative (or, at any rate, have a good idea of what it is), you can explain what will happen to him if he doesn't make the deal with you. Again, there's no need to be nasty or threatening about this, but explain coolly and logically why it's in his best interests to conclude the agreement.

Above all, remember that your ultimate weapon in a negotiation is your willingness to walk away from it. This has particular force in the end game, because your opponent has invested a lot in this discussion and doesn't want to see it go to waste. You need to be very clear at this stage in explaining what will cause you to walk away from the deal.

Let's look at an example:

SALES SCENARIO

Salesperson: We're coming right down to it here. I need to know from you if you're willing to take a one-year warranty on the product rather than three years.

Customer: No. I just can't accept a one-year guarantee. Couldn't we do two years?

Salesperson: No, I'm sorry. I understand your position, but that's not acceptable to us. If you stick with anything

> more than one year, I'm afraid there's no point in continuing the discussion.
>
> **Customer:** Well, maybe we can live with one year. But there'll have to be some give on the price.
>
> **Salesperson:** Let's talk about that.

In this example, the salesperson explains that the warranty is not something he's willing to yield on. He says explicitly that if they can't reach accommodation on this point, he'll walk away from the negotiation. That puts the ball in the customer's court—does he concede on this point (which he does), or does he also walk away from the discussion.

Clearly, each of you is going to have a different set of walkaway points. Part of your job in the first and middle parts of the negotiation is to figure out what those points are for your opponent. What will make him walk away? And what's he willing to negotiate further on? Once you decide that, you're ready for a successful end game.

The Real Deal

1. The object of the "middle game" in a negotiation is to determine your opponent's strengths and weaknesses and to clear away any extraneous issues that might get in the way of making the deal.
2. In the "end game" stage, you must resolve the outstanding issues, which will be the most important ones in the agreement, using a variety of tactics to win.
3. Your most powerful weapon in the end game negotiation is your willingness to walk away from the talks.

CHAPTER 19

The Devil's in the Details

A sales rep I know was elated beyond belief. This guy was practically dancing around the office as he told his colleagues how he'd held firm in his last negotiation and gotten some zingers through on the contract he'd inked with a client. The client had faxed a copy of the signed contracts, and the rep had passed them along to his supervisor for review.

After a while, his boss came out of the office where he'd been examining the signed contracts. "Could I see you a minute?" he asked the guy.

The salesperson walked in, a bounce in his step, expecting a mild reprimand for making too much noise and disrupting people's work. Instead, his boss thrust the signed copy of the contract at him.

"Have you read this?" he asked.

The rep looked at the clause to which his boss was pointing. He read it once, twice, and shook his head. He flipped to the last page of the contract. There was his signature all right.

"I'm sorry," he said. "I don't know how this got by me."

"I don't know either," his boss said grimly. "We've got to live with it now, but it means we're almost certainly going to lose money on this deal. And that's going to be very tough to explain to the front office. So you'd better have some kind of explanation when they're out here next week."

The story doesn't have a happy ending; I'll let you imagine for yourselves what the sales rep had to say to the higher ups about the deal he'd blown. But the whole affair, sad as it is, illustrates another important point about negotiations: You have to pay attention to the details.

He Who Writes, Wins

In any negotiation, there's a big advantage to being the person who writes the final contract. This will give you the upper hand, because when it comes down to it, contracts are words, and the person who writes the final words has the advantage. You can shape the precise terms of the agreement to your liking, and you can make sure nothing slips by you.

I think most people involved in negotiations are honest. But that doesn't stop them from trying to get the best deal possible. After all, that's their job. And it's your job when you're negotiating to pay attention to every last detail of the contract. Because once your signature (or that of your boss) goes on it, you'll have to carry it out.

At my company, we were in negotiations over a compensation package that we had offered to a salesperson I wanted to hire. We went back and forth about it, but in the end, we were able to hammer out a deal. Furthermore, our lawyers wrote the final agreement that everyone signed. That meant it was ten times more favorable than if the salesperson and his representative had drawn up the papers. I don't mean to imply here that we were trying to pull a fast one. My point is simply that the papers set out an agenda. And under all circumstances, it's best if you write the agenda.

Contracts are complicated things, and these days, with more and more lawyers getting involved in the simplest negotiation, they're even more complicated than when I started out in the business.

It won't do to skim the contracts at the time of signing. In fact, it's best if you can read through them when you're completely free of distractions and can dwell on the meaning of every word and phrase.

Don't rush reading the final contract for a deal.
Take your time.

Watch for Unintended Consequences

When you're looking at the details of a negotiation, especially at the final agreement that's going to come out of it, you have to assume that all the parties involved understand their best interests and are going to act on them. It won't do you any good after a deal is signed to say, "Oh, I didn't really mean that part. Can't we just forget we agreed on that?" If you accidentally agreed to something that's in the interests of your opponent, she or he isn't going to give it back to you.

A second point here is this: *When you're coming to a final agreement, assume the worst possible scenario.* This tactic grows out of what's called the Law of Unintended Consequences. Simply put, this law says that action you take on purpose will produce unexpected results.

In the '50s and '60s, city planners noticed that traffic congestion in big cities was getting worse. More and more people were able to afford cars and were driving them to more places.

The urban planners assumed—pretty reasonably, you'll have to admit—that since people were driving more, they'd need more roads. More roads would mean fewer cars per road and would help relieve the congestion. The result was a great burst of road building. In my home, New York City, urban planner Robert Moses launched a massive series of controversial highway-building projects.

However, when the highways were built, not only did they not relieve congestion, but also traffic was worse than ever. Drivers experienced backups that lasted for hours, with all the attendant frustration.

What happened?

The planners failed to foresee that creating more streets would encourage people to purchase and drive more cars. The number of cars on the road expanded to meet the availability of places to drive them. And the traffic problem got worse instead of better.

The point here is that in any agreement you make, there are going to be unintended consequences. Before you sign the deal, sit down and think through all the things that could go wrong if you sign the deal. Not that you shouldn't sign it, but you have to be ready for some of the unintended outcomes it will give rise to.

Some of these you'll be able to anticipate in the contract's language. Some you won't. But the more thought you give to the language of the deal, the better prepared you'll be.

Small details can have big consequences. Some ambiguity about delivery or an escalating discount can cost your company hundreds of thousands of dollars. Be sure to get the small stuff right, and there's a better chance you'll ace the big stuff as well.

The Real Deal

1. Try to control who writes the final agreement, since this will give you the most say over its details.
2. Read every contract very carefully; after it's signed, it has legal force.
3. Think through what the contract says *will* happen and what you imagine *might* happen as a result of signing it. Apply the Law of Unintended Consequences and think about worst-case scenarios so you can anticipate them in the contract's language.

CHAPTER 20

How to Win, How to Lose

"Winning," famed football coach Vince Lombardi said, "isn't everything. But the will to win is everything." Every salesperson should keep that quote on a card in her or his pocket and take it out just before walking into a negotiation. Because it sums up exactly what I've been talking about in this book.

You can't win unless you believe in your product or service and unless you believe in yourself.

If you follow the advice I've given you in this book, you'll better position yourself to win negotiations. Not all the time—no one can do that—but most of the time. And it's important that when the chairs are pushed back and everyone stands up and stretches and shakes hands, you know when you've won and when you've lost. It's equally important that you know how to behave under both those circumstances.

I've known some great negotiators in my time, people who knew how to put together complicated deals with dozens of moving parts, all working in harmony to produce the result they wanted. But one of their biggest tests as negotiators was not only how they behaved while they were striking a bargain but what they acted like afterward.

SALES SCENARIO

Three or four years ago, I was present when a sales rep finished up a negotiation. It had been a very tough slog, and it had taken several days. There were times when it looked as if the whole deal was going to fall apart. In the end, the rep got a deal, but it wasn't nearly what he wanted.

When he and the client put their signatures on the contract, the client stuck out his hand with some innocuous comment about how it had been a good, hard session but he was glad they'd arrived at an agreement.

The rep barely touched the outstretched hand, didn't look the client in the face, let his shoulders slump, and gave an incoherent grunt. Then he slouched out of the room without saying goodbye.

The client just stood staring after him with his mouth open.

Losing's Not the End of the World

Losing a deal is never pleasant, but letting it affect your whole attitude, as the rep in the story I just told you did, makes the situation ten times worse. Let's look at what happened.

First, even though the rep didn't get everything he wanted, *he got the sale.* That is, he got something rather than nothing. So he had that much to celebrate, at least.

Second, he made his defeat seem personal, as if somehow it was a comment on him and his abilities. By walking the borderline of rude with his customer, he raised doubts in the client's mind about how serious he could be about holding up his end of the bargain. Behavior such as he exhibited spoke volumes about how well this deal was likely to go.

If someone you just struck a complex deal with behaved like that, would you trust them or the company they represented? Would you want to do business with them again?

I didn't think so.

SCHIFFMAN SAYS . . .

No matter how a negotiation ends—whether you won or lost or a bit of both—look straight at your opponent, smile, grip his hand firmly, and shake it. You're not just concerned with this negotiation, after all. You're building a future with this person.

If you lose a deal, don't act like you lost. Act like you want to win the next deal. And you probably will.

On some level, negotiation is about perception. And the last thing you want to be perceived as is a loser. If you look defeated, the next time you sit across the table from your opponent, she'll know about how you react to setbacks. And she can use that information to push you further in the negotiation.

Be a Gracious Winner

If it's bad to be a sore loser, it's equally bad to be a vindictive or boastful winner. In truth, the best kind of win for you is going to be if you can align your interests and those of your client so that you both benefit from the deal you're putting together. But there are many points in any negotiation where you definitely want to come out in the best position, often at the expense of the person you're negotiating with. Those range from getting the client to agree to a higher price for your product to convincing him to take a new line of widgets from you.

This means that it's quite possible your opponent will realize that he's lost—he paid more than he intended or wound up getting products he didn't really want. If you try to rub in the fact that you accomplished what you set out to do in the session, chances are that he'll turn sullen or angry, and your relationship will be imperiled.

I keep saying, for you winning ultimately means *getting the sale*. And not just now but in the future. Why risk your client's goodwill for the sake of some cheap crowing because he agreed to pay a price that's higher than the one your last client agreed to?

If you've won, be nice about it. Point out to your opponent the benefits to him or her. Immediately follow up with practical suggestions for implementation, so the other party knows how enthusiastic you are about this deal.

Once again, body language is important. Firm, purposeful movements convey a sense of confidence and control. Always look your client full in the face when you're speaking to her, and never allow yourself to do anything or say anything that could be interpreted as gloating. (One rep I know, after closing a deal, remarked to his client, "Man, I was afraid you were going to hold out for a much lower number." The client looked at him for a moment then said, "Next time I will." And he did.)

Just because the negotiation itself is over doesn't mean you've ended the relationship with the other party. In fact, most of the time the negotiation is just the opening step in developing that relationship.

When you get back to the office after concluding a negotiation, write a follow-up note to your client. She or he will appreciate the consideration.

Winning is about substance, of course. But it's also important that you frame your win in such a way that your boss and your company and the company's shareholders understand what you won. As much as possible, you should also try to help your client achieve the same thing. When both sides understand what they've won, they'll be best able to act upon it.

The Value of Compromise

The most likely scenario in any negotiation is that neither party will entirely win or lose. You'll give on some points and get on others. Sometimes the talks may take a turn that neither of you anticipated, and you'll find a solution that makes both of you happy. Calvin (of *Calvin and Hobbes*) once remarked with the cynicism of a six-year-old, "A good compromise leaves everybody mad." Actually, in my experience a good compromise is one that leaves both parties thinking they got what they needed.

If you've established your objectives and your Alternative before you start the negotiation, you should be able to easily recognize whether a compromise is going to work for you. It may well be that by conceding on nonessential points, you'll win the big issue that's important to you.

You should welcome compromise as a useful way to get something from a negotiation. Don't worry if you have to let go of some small points. After all, you can try to regain them the next time you're negotiating with the client. It may well be that with the passage of time you'll come to realize they weren't as important as you thought they were.

Finally, you need to recognize when to shut up. I've already mentioned this in the first part of this book when I was talking about asking questions. But in the latter part of negotiations, there comes a time when you've won all you're going to win. That's the time to stop picking at the issues, smile, and reach your hand across the table to close the deal.

The Real Deal

1. Even if you didn't get everything you wanted from a deal, *act positive.* That will open the door for a better solution later on.

2. If you win—especially if you win more than you expected—don't gloat. Emphasize how good the deal is for the other party as well.

3. Look for compromises that make both sides happy.

CHAPTER 21

Coming Back to the Table

It's possible—I've done this myself on more than one occasion—that in the middle of a particularly tough negotiation you've gotten up, stalked to the door, told the other party what you think of them and their organization, and walked out. Emotionally, there's something deeply satisfying about slamming a door. It closes out all the negative energy bubbling and frothing on the other side and puts a barrier between it and you.

If you've done this, chances are you said to yourself, "Well, at least I never have to see *those people* again!"

And then—which has also happened to me—something happened. Maybe your boss decided you had to reopen talks. Maybe the relationship of forces between your two organizations shifted somehow. Whatever the case, you found yourself sitting at a table, the same group of faces staring back at you, and they were all smirking.

Never, you discovered, is a very, very long time.

It's quite possible, of course, that the negotiations to which you're returning ended on a much friendlier note. Sometimes it's possible to walk away from talks with both sides leaving open the possibility of resuming them in the future. In this chapter, I'll look at both scenarios. But there are some general rules that apply in any case where you're starting over again:

- **Don't have preconceptions.** The world hasn't stood still since you last spoke to the people who are now sitting on the other side of the table. A lot has happened, both in your organization and theirs. Their objectives have probably shifted, as have yours. So you need to start by determining what's now important to them. And the way to do that? You guessed it. Start asking questions.

- **Put the past away.** If this negotiation is going to go anywhere, you can't keep letting your mind go back to the time when the guy you're talking to dissed you or made you feel two feet tall. You can't keep looking backward and expect to walk ahead.

- **Don't forget the past.** This may seem to contradict what I just said, but it really doesn't. You don't need to focus on all the bad moments of your past negotiation. But you shouldn't start with a completely clean slate either, because that would mean you didn't learn anything. If this negotiator's style is to try to push your buttons, remember it. If she has certain hot buttons, remember what they are.

- **Be honest, and assume your client is honest until proven otherwise.** Whatever may have happened in your previous talks, start with the idea that you both want to win and that your goals overlap enough to make a solution possible. When you ended the discussion before, you may not have felt that way. But if a solution isn't possible, there's no point in reopening the negotiation.

Making the First Move

I was once involved in talks with a company to set up a training program. We got some distance in working out the details, but one day Chris, the executive with whom I'd been in discussions, came into the conference room with a long face. "Steve," he said, "I'm sorry, but our budget's been cut and I just don't have the money for this anymore."

I made an effort to persuade him that a training program for his sales force would have a significant revenue return for the company, but when he couldn't or wouldn't agree, I simply told him we'd pick things up again when his budget improved. I made a point of phoning him on a regular basis, passing the time, letting him know I was still interested in training his salespeople.

Finally, I read in the newspaper that Chris's company was the subject of a possible acquisition by a much larger company. I saw my opportunity and called him. I suggested to him that since the acquiring company would unquestionably be looking at his sales numbers and his salespeople, it would make the company more attractive if they could point to a training program they already had in place. Chris agreed, and we started our negotiations the following week.

Especially when your negotiations have broken off on a friendly note, it's to your advantage to make the first move to reopen them.

- It puts you in control of the negotiation.
- It demonstrates your desire to make the deal.

■ Psychologically, it makes you appear the stronger of the two parties.

When you first begin your talks again, it's important that you start by taking note of what's changed. Remember, it's not only possible, it's probable that your client's objectives have been altered, so you need to acknowledge this. If you try to start from exactly the point at which you broke things off, you'll be disappointed.

SCHIFFMAN SAYS . . .

Never forget that you're talking to people. The person on the other side of the table probably isn't that different from you. She has worries, pressures, and concerns, all of which have an impact on how she's negotiating.

Many times if you sense anger or confrontation, it's not directed at you but is a subconscious reflection of something else going on in her life.

Treat your opponent in negotiation with respect and consideration. It's about winning, not about whose ego is bigger.

In the case I mentioned above, when Chris and I sat down after our hiatus, the first thing I did was to ask him some questions about the acquisition. He told me that the acquiring company had used a different training program and they weren't very happy with it. Now I had a measure of comparison I could work with. So I asked him questions about the program, and we went, point by point, through why what I was offering was better. If I'd just tried to pick up where we left off, I'd have missed this very valuable opening.

After a Bad Breakup

A salesperson-client relationship can be like a marriage. There are ups and downs, good times and bad, and sometimes you just get on each other's nerves. In the worst cases, you divorce. Or, in the case of a business relationship, you stalk out of the negotiations and bang the door behind you.

How can you possibly come back to the table after that kind of scene? Believe me, it's not easy. I have as healthy an ego as the next person, and I don't like admitting I was hasty. So it's very wrenching to have to go back to the table when you swore you'd never talk to the other party.

But sometimes, like a marriage, a negotiation that seems dead can be saved. There are just a couple of points to concentrate on:

- Even though you may think it, never try to force the other party to say she or he was in the wrong. Every negotiation, whether we admit it to ourselves or not, is a little bit about ego. Nobody likes saying they were mistaken, and there's nothing to be gained from demanding such a confession. Instead, focus on the issues at hand, not what was said at the last session.

- Start by trying to get a consensus on what you agreed on already. In other words, go through the major points of convergence from your previous negotiation and make sure everyone's still okay with them. This will give you a framework for the rest of the discussion.

■ Watch out for the words, demands, attitudes, and anything else that derailed the negotiations last time. If you know your opponent is pushing your buttons, push back and let him know you know what he's doing. Above all, avoid a repeat of the behavior that led to the breakdown of the first negotiation.

Ideally, it's great if you can negotiate with different people, but that's not always possible. That's why you've got to, as much as you can, keep the personal out of the discussion. Remember that you don't have to like the client; you just have to do a successful deal with her or him.

The Real Deal

1. When resuming negotiations, don't obsess about the past, but don't forget it either.
2. Re-evaluate your objectives and those of your opponent so you get a fresh start in the discussions.
3. Whenever possible, try to restart negotiations with a different group of people, so the talks have a different dynamic than previously.
4. Never try to force anyone to say he or she was wrong.

CHAPTER 22

Some Final Thoughts

At the end of my book *Closing Techniques (That Really Work!)*, I listed "Eight Foundation Principles of Effective Negotiating." In case you've never read the book or have forgotten the principles, here they are:

1. The goal of negotiating is to end up with a better deal than could have been achieved without negotiating.
2. An effective daily prospecting routine improves your negotiating position.
3. To negotiate effectively, you must be able to identify the most important interests of each side.
4. To negotiate effectively, you must be able to develop creative options that allow both sides to broadcast a "win" to their constituents (boss, colleagues, shareholders, etc.).
5. To negotiate effectively, you must be able to identify an outcome that both sides will recognize as "fair."
6. "Knee-jerk" discounting of price is the lowest form of negotiation.

7. You must never enter a potential negotiating meeting without a backup plan.

8. The next best thing to actually negotiating from a position of strength is acting as though you are negotiating from a position of strength.

To one extent or another, I've revisited each of these points in this book. To them, I'd add a ninth—in some ways the most important.

9. Every negotiation is a dialogue.

As soon as you recognize the truth of that ninth point, you're well on your way to being an effective negotiator. Because the biggest mistake that salespeople make when they're negotiating a deal is to assume they're the only ones who can offer anything.

I started out with the story of my friend Bob, who simply sat in his chair without saying anything and by doing so, got a better deal on some windows. I chose that story because it's a great illustration of several mistakes many salespeople make when they begin a negotiation:

- **It's not always about price.** In fact, many times price is a relatively unimportant factor in your client's objectives. That's why it's such a big mistake to assume that "negotiate" means "discount."
- **You can't negotiate with yourself.** The salesperson didn't try to talk to Bob. Rather, he assumed he knew what Bob wanted and proceeded to talk himself into a 40 percent discount.

- **Step one is to find out what winning means to the other side**. If you don't know what your opponent wants out of the negotiation, you won't be able to win, because you won't know how to balance your interests against his and find the places where they line up together.

Don't Be Afraid of Failure

Someone—no one seems quite sure who—once said, "You must be fully prepared to lose a great deal in order to make a great deal."

I think that's true. In negotiation, as in just about everything else in life, if you're not prepared for some risk, you'll never reap the rewards.

One salesman spent a long time setting up a meeting with a vice president at a big company. He had to penetrate through about fifteen layers of corporate bureaucracy to talk to this guy. It involved more red tape than negotiating with the Kremlin, but he finally managed it. Before he went in to talk to the VP, his boss advised him not to push anything. Just get in and get the basic sale and get out, he said in effect.

During most of the meeting, the salesman stuck to this script, sketching out a short-term conservative deal. The final agreement was for an amount of money that was significant to the salesperson's company but was not very much relative to the size of the big company.

Finally, the vice president nodded and said, "Well, I think we're about done."

Clearly, this was a sign that the meeting was at an end. But the salesperson thought back on all the time he'd spent to set this up and all the energy he'd invested in this meeting. He squared his shoulders and said, "There's one other thing.

I think we're thinking too small here. We don't want to continually be negotiating with each other. I'd like to extend the agreement we've just made to a five-year contract, with the option to renew it at the end of that five years."

The executive looked at him in surprise. Then he sat down, smiled, and said, "Well, at least you were bold enough to ask. That's more than any of our other vendors have done."

They wound up striking a multiyear deal, far better than the original agreement they'd hammered out.

I'm not saying you should try this sort of thing all the time. Negotiation isn't something I like to fail at, and I try to keep my losses to a minimum. But I've learned as well that you can't be afraid of failure. Sometimes you have to ask for the stars and settle for the moon.

You and the person sitting across from you both want the deal to happen. If you didn't, one of you wouldn't be there. So when you're planning your battle, keep some long shots in mind, and if the atmosphere in the negotiation seems right, go for them.

In a previous book, *Sell Like the Best*, I said that very few people are "born salespeople." Great salespeople have skills that can and must be learned, and I believe that almost anyone, with some application, can learn them.

The same is true of negotiators. If you study the lessons in this book and practice, with experience and confidence you can become a world-class negotiator.

Good luck!

Index

About the Author

Stephan Schiffman has trained more than 500,000 sales-people at firms such as AT&T Information Systems, JP Morgan Chase, Motorola, and U.S. Healthcare. Mr. Schiffman, founder and chairman of DEI Management Group, is the author of *Cold Calling Techniques (That Really Work!)*, *The 25 Sales Habits of Highly Successful Salespeople*, and several other popular books on sales.

Do you have questions, comments, or suggestions regarding this book? Please share them with me! Write to me at this address: *sschiffman@steveschiffman.com.*

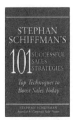